Stoic Six Pack 5:
The Cynics

Stoic Six Pack 5:
The Cynics

By

Diogenes Laërtius

John MacCunn

Publius Syrus

and

Xenophon

Enhanced Media
2015

Stoic Six Pack 5 – The Cynics

An Introduction to Cynic Philosophy by John MacCunn. Originally published as *The Cynics* by John MacCunn in 1904.

The Moral Sayings of Publius Syrus, a Roman Slave by Publius Syrus. Translated by Darius Lyman. First published in 1856.

Life of Antisthenes, Life of Diogenes and *Life of Crates* by Diogenes Laërtius. From *The Lives and Opinions of Eminent Philosophers* by Diogenes Laërtius. Translated by Charles Duke Yonge. First published in 1853.

The Symposium: Book IV by Xenophon. From *The Collected Works of Xenophon in Four Volumes*. Translated by H. G. Dakyns. Published in 1890.

Stoic Six Pack 5 – The Cynics

Published by Enhanced Media.

Enhanced Media Publishing
Los Angeles, CA.

First Printing: 2015.

ISBN 978-1-329-74375-5

Contents

An Introduction to Cynic Philosophy

By

John MacCunn

"Other dogs," said Diogenes, punning upon the designation of his School, "bite their enemies: I bite my friends for their salivation"; and it may be confidently affirmed that he and his friends were admirably fitted for the friendly office. Gifted with impressive intellectual force, with unbounded capacity of contempt, and with a pungent humor, they did not know how to spare either men or institutions. The retort of Diogenes to his fellow citizens of Sinope is typical. He was told that they had condemned him to banishment. "And I," was the rejoinder, "condemn them—to live in Sinope."

The attitude of Diogenes to the men of Sinope was the attitude of the Cynic school to society at large. Like most ascetic systems it had its roots, in part at least, in revolt against the world. Nothing pleased them. With a trenchant dichotomy, they divided mankind into the handful of wise men and innumerable fools.

"Of what am I guilty," once exclaimed Antisthenes, "that I should be praised?"

And the words came well from one to whom popularity was but "the babble of madmen." Even the most cherished ideas of the Athenian served only to point corrosive retort. Was it civic patriotism? "Why should I be proud of belonging to the soil of Attica with the worms and the slugs?" Was it the war-like spirit—that spirit that Plato, even in his idealized Greek state, weds so closely to philosophy? "Let a man apply himself to philosophy till he has come to regard the leaders of armies as the drivers of asses." Was it popular election? (The Athenians, it will be remembered, were so democratic that they elected even their generals). "They might as well nominate their asses to be horses." So all along the line. Political institutions, property, the family, luxury in all modes, culture at least in many aspects —all serve but as targets for Cynic projectiles. Even the Athenian attachment to ceremonial religion—so singularly tenacious despite all the free thought of the Sophistic era—finds short shrift in the blunt declaration that a temple is no holier than any-other place.

It might seem that views like these have at any rate the merit of being unambiguous. And it would not do to accuse the Cynics of saying anything they did not think, or of thinking anything they did not say. Yet for this very reason there is possibility of misconception. This in two directions. For we must not take these Cynic utterances too solemnly. The Cynics were philosophers; but they were also satirists and humorists. Like all the masters of vituperation, they had a zest in the commination service. And this being so, it would betray a lack of humor to read all these flings, flouts, sneers, sarcasms, as if they were meant for philosophic formulae. Once, it appears, Diogenes was shown some ingenious kind of dial; "Not a bad contrivance," was the rejoinder, "to avoid missing one's meals." We make take this seriously if we like. But it may be safer to put it alongside of Antisthenes' asseveration (wrung from him possibly in some moment of exasperation with dilettantism) that "a wise man will not learn to read so as not to be troubled by trifles." One must beware of the pedantic literalism of the men who cannot laugh.

For two reasons any such misinterpretation would be grossly unjust, (a) One that the Cynic revolt against society was far from unprovoked. In our gratitude for what Greece has done for us (and what has it not done for us?), we must not forget that even the Greece of Pericles had its blots. It was devastated by constant wars, and it could be ruthless in its manner of waging them. It was split up into little municipal states which hated each other with a perfect hatred, as Athens hated Thebes or Sparta, or as Thebes hated Athens. It was built upon slavery —the horrible slavery of the mines as well as the milder bondage of the household; and it grew into slavery rather than out of it. Beautiful in so much, even as its own Parthenon, Greek civilization could as little assimilate this servile substratum as could the Parthenon transmute into frieze and columns the native rock of the Acropolis. And then these little States were torn by those intestine rivalries, and cursed by those unscrupulous ambitions which led to the political inferno described in lurid pages by Thucydides. Add to this the perennial vices that may only too surely be reckoned upon where wealth has grown, and luxury increased, and command of leisure and facilities for culture borne their usual harvest of dilettantism. Who will say that such a society did not need its censors and satirists? There was a word of advice once given by Diogenes. It may be commended to all those, whether individuals or nations, who wince under the lash of their critics: "Associate with your enemies: they will be the first to tell you of your faults." The second point—the second consideration which forbids us to take Cynicism too lightly—is that, despite all its extravagances it rested on a principle. Disgust with social life was part of it. But it was not the main part, nor would it ever have been so bitter had it not found inspiration elsewhere in the life, and in the doctrine, of Socrates.

It sometimes happens that a great man, though himself far enough from being sectarian, becomes the founder of sects. He cannot help it. He is so great that his followers, being lesser men, and quite unable to see around him, come to mistake the part for the whole, to fashion their god in their own imperfect image, and to subsist each of them upon his own favorite fragment of the master's example and teaching. This, at least, was what happened to Socrates. None of the world's great thinkers has ever gathered into discipleship men of such varied types; and never did philosopher trouble himself less than did this philosophic genius to keep all his utterances formally consistent, or to hand on to successors the doubtful legacy of a dogmatic system. The result followed. When he passed away, it was Plato alone who reproduced him in his splendid many-sidedness. For the rest, the varied aspects of truth that had found unity in the Socratic personality fell asunder into fragments, which were portioned out among followers who, as usual, all claimed the true apostolic succession, and all repudiated every succession but their own. Hence arose those schools so fitly called the incomplete Socratics; and among them, arrogant in their incompleteness, the Cynics.

When Antisthenes, the founder of the school, first made the acquaintance of Socrates, he could hardly have appeared a promising disciple. He was already middle-aged, "too old to learn." He was himself already a teacher of philosophy; and who does not know that for a man to have disciples is by no means the surest way to become a disciple himself? Yet Antisthenes was not deterred. We see him, cross-grained and cantankerous though he seems to have been, tramping his five miles from the Peiraeus to meet with Socrates in the Agora, and to learn from his lips the open secrets of a deeper philosophy. And then there was so much in Socrates that came half way to meet his admiration. For Socrates was anything but the typical Greek. He was rugged and plain. His dress was coarse. His manner of life was frugal. He was an admirable campaigner. Hunger and thirst, cold winds and scorching suns, could make no impression on that iron frame. He often went barefoot. And though he could enjoy himself in due season—witness The Symposium of Plato—he could also be abstemious to asceticism. Nor was he fastidious in his company. Rich men and poor came much alike to him. And as for his talk, it was not at all of the kind that the Greeks, or most of us since, have been accustomed to hear from philosophers. For it seemed to deal little with the high themes of the schools, with the cosmologies of the early philosophers, or with the abstract science of some of his contemporaries. Has not Zeller even called him "philistine"? In truth, there were men who, when they met him, were shocked to find to what an extent his conversation ran upon smiths, tailors, tanners, saddlers, and such like. And though in this homely talk, in these analogies, thrice-vulgar to Greek ears, there lay in germ nothing less than the idealism of Plato, this did not appear upon the surface.

There were remarks, too, which must have found in Antisthenes a receptive soil. "To need nothing is divine, to need as little as one can is all but divine." It was sayings like this that Antisthenes carried with him to bear their fruit in due season in Cynic life and doctrines. There were, of course, other sides to Socrates—urbanity, zest in the gaiety of life, humorous toleration for human weakness, reverence for the laws of the land, a profound religious spirit. But Antisthenes cared for none of these things. Enough for him that he had found a pattern of austerity, conviction, and rationality.

Yet it was not the character only of Socrates that wrought upon the Cynics. It was also his doctrine.

Socrates was not merely a moral philosopher. Like Plato and Aristotle after him, he was also, and even more, a moral reformer. For his lot was cast in an age of transition. The unsuspecting confidence of the morality of tradition was passing. Not all the forces of reaction, with Aristophanes to head them, could bring it back. Athens had turned that earlier page. The swift brilliant expansion of national greatness that followed the Persian war had brought new problems; and a widened horizon had opened Athenian eyes to the diversity and variability of moral standards. Not least, there was at work the searching solvent of those great thinkers of the Attic illumination— the Sophists. In their hands a rhetorical sensationalism was raising doubts as to the possibility of knowledge of an objective moral order; and a rhetorical egoism in ethics rapidly preparing the way for an identification of right with might, of law with force, of obligation with fear, of justice with a perishable and changing thing of human institution. Can it be wondered at if there were those who feared that before this the very props of moral and political obligation were going, and that an urgent practical need called for a supreme effort of reconstruction. Among these were the great constructive thinkers of Greece.

Two courses lay open. The one was to recognize the organic dependence of morality upon social conditions; and in the light of that, to attack the vast problem of reconstructing society upon a more rational basis. This was the way of Plato and Aristotle. But it was not the way of Socrates. In the eyes of Socrates the one vital reform was the reform of individual men. And the needful specific was of the simplest. It was what has now become the good old way of hoisting scepticism with its own petard, of meeting the critical and sceptical reason by appeal to reason that was critical and not sceptical. This was the way of Socrates. In season, and sometimes out of season, he insisted that morality stood or fell simply with the possibility of bringing men to think, or (to be more precise) of bringing them to clear, well-defined, and sound ideas of what their duties were. As all the world knows, he taught that virtue is knowledge. And though an exact interpretation of the formula is far from easy, the dictum meant (and this is what concerns us) that, if the moral life is to be set upon a sure basis, it must be through the enlightening of the will—the will which, to Socrates, as to the Stoics, to Spinoza, to Kant, meant the reason of the individual.

It was here the Cynics laid hold. One may not say they reproduced their master. It is evident that reason in their eyes had not the same function as in his. There was less of knowledge, less emphasis on definitions. There was more of simple strength of rational personal conviction. But on one point there was entire agreement, on the vital point that, in things moral, it is the spirit that profiteth, or, as Antisthenes. has it, that "men are rich and poor not in their establishments, but in their souls." No philosopher of either the ancient or the modern world, not even Kant, has so insisted that in comparison with the good will all else is as dross.

It was in fact just this which led them to leave their master far behind. In identifying virtue with the enlightened or rational will, Socrates had made virtue inward. But he had never meant that, therefore, virtue was not outward. On the contrary, he had frankly accepted the life of Athens as he found it. He had done his duty as a citizen on the field and in the dicastery. He had submitted himself to the laws, even when they adjudged him to die. And in giving his life to the mission of personally influencing individuals, he had taken it for granted that the men he dealt with were, like himself, living the ordinary civic life of the average Athenian. Not so the Cynics.

Seizing upon the truth that virtue is, in its essence, inward (a state of will or reason), they went on to infer that, therefore, it must not be outward; and in that uncompromising spirit declared that there is no true moral life for man till he has cut himself loose from every tie, every resource, every institution which social life has to offer.

They had a certain justification. "He who hath a wife and children hath given hostages to fortune." Extend the trite aphorism and we have Cynicism in a nutshell. Not wife and children alone, but friends, wealth, reputation, public position, institutions, all things on which men have set their hearts—are they not all "hostages to fortune" ? For all ordinary life is at best precarious. It is precarious even by reason of its outward resources, which, whatever security they may bring, do, as a matter of fact, in proportion as they widen the range of interests, offer thereby a larger target to the slings and arrows of misfortune, and stake our happiness upon eventualities beyond our own control. There is but one effectual security. Care for none of these things. Give never a hostage to fortune. Minimize wants even to the vanishing point. Be independent.

"Rally the good in the depth of thyself."

Such is the message of the Cynics. All external goods were in their eyes obstructions, all social interests distractions, all dependence, whether on men or on things, an impediment, a sacrifice of the soul's 'self-sufficingness.' Like the Stoics when they asserted their freedom in the last abnegation of suicide; like the Christian anchorites when they sought for their own souls in the desert; like the monks when they strove for spirituality of life in the austerities of the cloister; like the begging-friars who raised mendicancy into an article of their faith, so did these Cynics turn their backs upon all the world had to offer, in the conviction that this was the path to moral victory. "He taught me," said Diogenes, of Antisthenes, "what was mine and not mine. Property was not mine. Kith and kin, acquaintances, friends, fame, intimate associates, places of abode, occupation— all these he taught were no concern of mine. What then was thine? The exercise of my own thoughts. This I might possess unhindered."

This result is even more apparent if we glance from the Cynic doctrine to the Cynic life. The typical figure is of course Diogenes. When he came to Athens, it appears he had a slave who ran away. The owner's consolation was peculiar: "If Manes can do without Diogenes, so, surely, can Diogenes without Manes." This was the keynote of all his long life. It is all a progressive discovery of how many things he can do without, a prolonged process of self-denudation. It went on till his death, which was characteristic. His friends found him one morning lying on the stones of one of those porticos which were his usual sleeping place. They thought him asleep. But he had in truth at last achieved the final minimization of wants.

We can now perhaps understand how the two aspects of Cynicism stand related. There was the revolt against society; there was the conviction inspired by Socrates that the seat of virtue is the rational will. These two joined hands in the lifelong struggle after a moral independence, an individual self-sufficingness, which carried in it an affirmation at once of the supreme moral worth of life, and of the worthlessness of everything that life had to offer.

If we are to do justice to this strange and picturesque philosophy we must not dwell too much upon its externals. Ascetics are never to be judged by the singularity of their austerities; and in this case rags, filth, and indecency must not obscure the fact that Cynicism was the first thorough-going plea for moral freedom which the western world had seen. In this aspect it is in advance even of Plato and Aristotle. For these, though by far the greatest ethical thinkers of the ancient world, have yet their limitations. To both of them, the moral life is still identified with the peculiarly Greek form of civic organization. It is so even in the ideal republic of Plato, which is, after all, no more than the Greek state glorified. Hence that intense civic exclusiveness persistent even in Platonic and Aristotelian ideals, to which the larger unities, national or cosmopolitan, were hardly yet above the horizon. Hence the profoundly aristocratic spirit even of the municipal so-called democracies; and hence, too, the basal institution of slavery of which the great philosophers were the apologists. These limitations were, in time, to disappear, and it needed other forces besides theory to demolish them. But it is to the credit of the Cynics to have declared, and that while the way was still in full vitality, that the moral life of the individual did not stand and fall with Greek civilization. They were cosmopolitans when as yet the Christian and Stoic cosmopolitanism was a long way off. Nor had they anything of the aristocratic leanings of Plato. Far from it; "philosophers of the proletariat" they were, after their own fashion, men with a mission who were convinced that philosophy had its message to the multitude—the multitude whom Plato declared to be inherently incapable of philosophy. And as they were certainly no respecters of persons, to them the barriers between bond and free, so insurmountable even to Aristotle, were broken down. Nor is it easy to exaggerate the importance to ethical thought of the idea upon which all this indifference to externals rested; the conviction that in all moral estimates it is the good will that is alone significant. It was a doctrine which was peculiarly needed in Greece. For where—as in Athens—private life and public life were so intimately related, and where the individual found free and satisfying expression for himself in political activities, as well as in attainable enjoyment of the best literature and art, there was a risk that the inward life might receive less than its due. Lives that find a quite congenial environment are apt to lack something of spiritual intensity. And though it might be maintained that the antidote was already there in the teaching of Socrates, and the deepening of the moral consciousness which it involved, it may be doubted whether, without Cynic exaggeration of Socratic doctrine, Plato and Aristotle would have laid such impressive stress upon the spirit in which an action is done as the supreme condition of its goodness. It is a lesson that has never been lost. Caught up by the Stoic philosophy, and incarnated in the Stoic life, it became one of the great legacies of ancient thought to modern ethics.

Nor is it to be denied that even the Cynic gospel of self-detachment from social life rests on a truth. We are all in some sense monads, self-centred in our being, however manifold our relations to others. Our thoughts, our hopes, our fears, our sorrows, all our experiences, are in a very peculiar sense our own. "It seems to me," says Sir J. F. Stephen, "that we are spirits in prison, able only to make signals to each other, but with a world of things to think and to say which our signals cannot describe at all." Or, as Wordsworth has it—

"Points have we all within ourselves
Where each stands single."

And, indeed, it is something of a common-place that when the world—even our own intimate world—has done its utmost for us, a limit is reached in every grave crisis beyond which we must be ourselves or succumb. It is but a half-truth perhaps. But then it was precisely the strength of the Cynics to belong to that order of one-sided minds without which mankind would never know what whole truths mean.

Mankind, however, and more especially philosophic mankind, are never content to live long upon half-truths. They have an irresistible tendency to pass to the other halves. And it is a striking comment upon this text that when Antisthenes was declaring that he had rather be mad than feel pleasure, Aristippus was maintaining the supreme end of life to be the pleasure of the moment. Hence that line of criticism which sets itself to show that Cynicism does but scant justice to the volume and variety of human life.

This, however, is perhaps beyond our limits. It must suffice at present to point out that, taking these Cynics upon their own ground, the manner of life they praised and practiced was anything but well fitted to compass the end they so strenuously laid to heart.

For, in an evil hour for their own cause, they turned their backs upon speculative philosophy. This was the more perverse in that Socrates had suggested a better way. For though Socrates was not himself a speculative philosopher, his ethical teaching had opened the way for a metaphysic. His life-long labor was a search after definitions of our moral concepts and categories; and the pre-supposition of this great effort was the conviction that these concepts, these definitions, had an objective ground in the nature of things. Hence it came about that his philosophy left as legacy to the speculative genius of Plato the epoch-making problem of finding a metaphysic of morals. Now with Socrates the Cynics went a certain length. To them, as to him, morality spelt reason, and reason meant moral conviction. But then, in their case, this moral conviction, as so often happens with ascetics, lacked "content." How could they pass on to the Socratic task of defining the concrete virtues— justice, temperance, bravery, and the rest—when they were spending all their lives in flinging contempt on those relations of social life in which, and through which, these, and all other virtues, could alone gain "content" and actuality? Add to this that, in their excessive preoccupation with the moral life, they came to regard speculative philosophy as an intellectual luxury, or, in other words, as but one of the modes of culture which fell under their ban. It fits with this that, in such speculative excursions as they did make—and Antisthenes had enough of the thinker to indulge these up to a point—their results only served to accentuate this divergence from the fruitful Platonic development of Socrates. For Antisthenes was a thorough-going nominalist, and as such stood committed to the anti-Platonic doctrine that all general concepts, be they of the virtues or of things in nature, are no more than general terms without objective counterparts or confirmatory realities in the nature of things. This blocked for him effectually the path that led Plato, in his development of Socratic teaching, to his metaphysical doctrine of a cosmos of "ideas" in which all general concepts, whether ethical or scientific, find their objective ground. Small wonder then if Antisthenes disparaged speculative thought when thus, in his eyes, it had become barren.

It is not our present concern to examine the value of this nominalistic doctrine. Our object is simply to point out that, in the interests of Cynic morality, nothing could have been more fatal. For, by this disparagement of the speculative life, the Cynics robbed themselves of what has ever been, and still is, one of the most effective of all pleas for the life of self-detachment from the world. Surely if man be ever justified in sitting loose to the life of institutions and the duties of citizenship, it is when he is possessed by a passion for scientific investigation or speculative truth. Not all the triflings of dilettantism can obscure the fact that a passion of this kind, if it be sincere, exacts an undivided allegiance. It is not simply that life is too short for anyone to do great things both in theory and practice. It is that the whole speculative and scientific attitude of mind is fundamentally diverse from that of the restless and crowded life of affairs. Plato saw this. He saw it, although no speculative thinker has ever been sterner than he in exacting social service of the philosopher. For Plato tells us also that, however strenuously the thinker must take the burden of the commonwealth on his shoulders, his heart and mind are really elsewhere, and ever ready to quit politics for that serene pursuit of truth in which his closing years are to be spent. And Aristotle follows Plato.

There is no mistaking the sharpness of the antithesis in which he sets the practical and the contemplative life, nor can words be more explicit than those in which, in the tenth book of "The Ethics," he tells us that, in proportion as a man rises to the life of thought, the less does he stand in need of those outward resources, and of that part-partnership in action with his fellow-citizens, without which the moral life is impossible. And, indeed, his words here and in the context have actually been pressed (falsely, but not unnaturally) into a plea for the life of retreat from the world. Surely then it was in an evil hour that the Cynics turned away from speculative thought. Even if they lacked the speculative instinct—and no doubt they did—they would still have been wise not to defraud themselves of this strongest of all arguments for detachment from the world. There have been quiet-ists, who have had little to show to the world for years which were filled with communion with their God. There have been thinkers, both in science and philosophy, whose epoch-making speculations have been only possible to men who, like Spinoza, lived remote and secluded. Who will say that theirs were empty lives? Yet this is what the Cynics missed. They abjured, they decried the life of citizenship—and for what?

This leads to a further criticism. For when philosophy or science demands self-dedication to the theoretic life, it is not barren of most practical results. It is of the very essence of it that it brings the finite individual life into conscious relation to a supreme Realty—call it Idea of the Good, Infinite Substance, the Absolute, Deussive Natura —which, in Spinoza's language, can fill the soul entirely. And it is because the individual, otherwise insignificant indeed, can turn to this alike in thought and in feeling, that he can become capable of the strength to lift himself above the shocks and cares and vanities about which those who have not seen the vision disquiet themselves in vain. Such at any rate has been the experience of most of the great prophets of individual independence. It was so with the Stoic sage, strong to defy the world because consciously at one with the reason which moves through all things. It was so with the Reformers and the Puritans, who resisted principalities and powers, not in their own strength, but "by grace." It was so with our own Carlyle, in whose eyes true self-reliance finds its ground, much as it did in his prototypes the Hebrew prophets, in unshaken trust in "the old eternal laws that live for ever." In all there is a gospel of self-sufficing-ness; and in all it is self-sufficingness through conscious dependence upon some supreme Reality that exists beyond the flux and commotion of human affairs.

From this source of strength the Cynics were cut off. In their struggle after an absolute moral independence, in their narrowly practical concentration upon this, they turned away, with fatal blindness, from the perennial sources of individual strength. So will it ever be with all who follow them in magnifying the moral life to the neglect or disparagement of a religious faith or a speculative philosophy.

Nor, quite apart from this, can one admit that their practical philosophy was the true path to that personal morality for which they were so ready to offer up, on a ruthless altar, all the world could give. One can see this in the later history of the school. With the passing of its great founders, Antisthenes and his disciple Diogenes, its inspiration seems to have left it. For, though the later Cynics kept up the old heroic tradition of plain living, their plain living gravitated downwards to unredeemed beggary, squalor, and indecency. They still, of course, flattered themselves that they possessed their own souls, but their souls, like those of many a raving anchorite in the desert, or fanatical Stylites on his pillar, could hardly be said to be worth the possessing. It is a well-known epigram of Aristotle that the solitary is either beast or god, and it is to be feared that these later Cynics had little of the god.

One cannot wonder. It was but the Nemesis that is so apt to overtake all votaries of an extreme asceticism which, in a leap after, the moral heroic, rashly renounces the homelier ordinary incentives to virtue. Such incentives, be it the love of home and kindred, the affection for friends, the kindliness of daily life, the honorable pursuit of wealth, the loyalty to an institution, the stimulus of public spirit, the love of country, these incentives may look commonplace beside the passion for saving souls, the heroic spirit of renunciation, the rupture of all ties, the hating of father and mother for the Kingdom of Heaven's sake. Yet it is at our peril that we try to cut out these incentives, and, like the Cynics, cast them from us. For, however, nobly the forlorn hope of morality may still struggle upwards by the way of renunciation, the risk is that the mass of mankind, bereft of the ordinary motives that are the permanent safeguards of morality, may find nothing to check their descent towards the brute.

This is what Aristotle saw with convincing clearness. Aristotle does not denounce the Cynics. In his usual tolerant and inclusive fashion he goes all the way with them in insisting that the moral life must be a thing complete and all-sufficing in itself. He adopts the very watchword of Cynicism, "self-sufficingness" - *abrapxeia*. But then the Aristotelian self-sufficingness is not of the sort that minimizes wants, and leaves the individual isolated from his kind and stripped of life's resources. On the contrary, it is the self-sufficingness which can only be won by the slow process of self-realization; and which sees in life's resources not clogs, not distractions, not hostages to fortune, but the instruments by whose right use alone human nature can develop its powers. It is all summed up in a single aphorism: "the state is the limit of self-sufficing-ness," meaning, that for a full and soul-satisfying life the "social animal," man, needs no less than all that is included in a well-organized society. This exactly hits the weakness of Cynic asceticism. So long as ascetics content themselves with railing at the world, they are not likely to fail of occupation. The crux comes when we ask, What next? Denunciation, renunciation, satire, negations however forcible, however witty, are impotent to develop the soul of the man who tries to subsist upon them. There is but one way—the way of Aristotle and of Carlyle—it is by finding one's work and doing it. For without a sphere of action the soul is irretrievably atrophied, and without a sphere adequate at least in some measure to the varied potentialities of man, the best gifts of the soul, which come by acting in the world, not by withdrawing from it in an impotent fancied superiority, will never be possessed. It was the paradox of Cynicism, as it is of many other forms of asceticism, that in a true antinomian fervor it at once magnified the moral life, and in the very act of doing so denied to it on the threshold the elementary conditions of its realization. For the wisdom of Aristotle here points the way not only to a fuller, more many-sided, and more beneficent life than the fanaticism of the "mad Socrates," Diogenes, but to a more than Cynic self-possession and a more than Cynic independence.

Nor it is to be granted that, even in its denunciations, Cynicism made war upon the world in the most effective way. Human nature will endure, and even welcome, satire and commination, especially when humorous. Satire is good reading, and the masters of invective, Juvenal, Swift, Carlyle, are far from unpopular. But there is nothing which so effectually turns the edge of invective as the perception that it is undiscriminating. We feel this about the diatribes of Antisthenes and the rest. They denounced war, but to what purpose, when we feel that they would have equally denounced a filibuster's raid and the civic devotion of Marathon or Salamis? They rose above the narrow exclusiveness were the first cosmopolitans; but what of that, when we feel sure that they would have risen above the kingdom of heaven could it have descended four-square upon earth? After an it is a spurious and an easy cosmopolitanism which comes of indifference to the fatherland. The true cosmopolitanism comes by antecedence, not by negation of patriotism. They protested, too, and vehemently enough, against Greek forms of ritual, but one feels that they would have swamped in one common condemnation the most devout achievements of religious art, and the mere antics of superstition. It is so all along the line. It is the easiest function in the world to object, if one has made up his mind to be always in opposition. It is also a role doomed to ineffectually. The Cynics, ancient or modern, who give us no credit for our ordinary virtues, will find us slow to give effect to their diatribes against our extraordinary vices. Their moral purpose may be excellent, "to bite us for our salvation." But it is not reasonable, it is subversive of all just gradations of moral value, and would not cure but kill, were we to don the staff and wallet of Diogenes, and turn this sharp medicine into the daily diet either of individuals or nations.

And yet, when all is said, it would ill befit us to fall in to a Cynic attitude towards Cynicism itself. Rather let us leave it with the reflection that, so long as philosophy has a message for mankind, Cynicism will stand as a memorable reminder that the spirit is more than the flesh, life of more value than its trappings, duty greater than pleasure, and the rational will strong enough to overcome the world.

The Moral Sayings of Publius Syrus

By

Publius Syrus

Translated by Darius Lyman

PREFACE

When *The Edinburgh Review* was established, the following motto was proposed for it: *Tenui musam meditamur avend.* The motto adopted reads as follows: *The judge is condemned, when the criminal is acquitted.*

This sentiment perhaps expressed the purpose of the Reviewers better than any other that could have been found—which was to bring to the trial of the public judgment, certain institutions of England, which if but once put on trial would most surely be condemned. Years since, I sought in vain for a copy of the work from which that motto was drawn. When at last a copy of Syrus came into my hands, it seemed strange that a writer of such wit and acuteness should not have been a great favorite with each of the Reviewers. That he was not, I could only account for by supposing that the original was seldom published by itself on account of its brevity; and that it was rarely translated, from the fact that many of the sayings derive their pith from the circumstance of their illustrating the character of personages represented in a play.

But whether the Edinburgh Reviewers knew much or little of Syrus, matters not. A writer whom these Reviewers had never read, who yet furnished their journal with a very appropriate motto, and with whom many of our popular proverbs originated, I here take the liberty to introduce to the people in a free English dress, knowing that if his noble shade is yet cognizant of his literary remains, he will thank me for bringing him before a public more capable of appreciating his good things than a Roman mob, and better able to practice his wiser moral precepts if so disposed, than most of the best of his contemporaries.

I would only bespeak the charity of the reader for the seeming insipidity to be found in some of the Sayings. As these were gleaned, after Syrus's day, from his Mimes or Plays, the compiler of them would be liable to such a mistake as he might make who should attempt to gather from the works of our great English dramatist a complete list of Shakespeare proverbs; that is, he would be likely to insert in his collection, many sayings which would be without meaning, except when taken in the proper connection of the play — and many maxims of doubtful morality, because originally fitted to the mouth of a Shylock; or an Iago.

Translator.

THE LIFE OF SYRUS

Time has wrought Syrus a singular destiny, building up for him a second reputation on the ruins of a first. Of his plays, which were the admiration of the Romans, the ages have brought down to us only a few sayings which were dispersed through them. The sayings were for that age of secondary consideration; they are now his chief performance. Thus deprived of the glory he once had, he has conquered another, and the once celebrated dramatist has become posterity's famous gnomic poet.

Like Terence and Phaedrus, Syrus passed his early years in slavery; but as we have no evidence that he was born a slave, it is supposed he became one, when Syria, his native country, was reduced to a Roman province by Pompey (year of Rome 690; 64 BC). He was brought to Rome when about twelve years of age, by an inferior officer of the army, called Domitius, as report goes, and thereupon received the name Syrus, in accordance with the custom by which slaves took a name derived from that of their province.

The young Syrian was fair, and well formed, of lively wit, and ready at repartee. Domitius taking him one day to the house of his patron to pay his court, as was a client's duty, the latter was struck with the elegance of his manners, and the beauty of his person — "an excellent recommendation," as Syrus himself has said, and particularly at Rome. The patron begged his little slave of Domitius, and the present was of course immediately made.

Syrus soon surprised his new master with sallies of wit superior to his age and condition. They were one day crossing a court together, in which a slave afflicted with the dropsy lay idly basking in the sun.

"What are you doing there?" cried the master in an angry tone.

"He is only warming his water," said Syrus; and the master's anger vanished in a laugh.

On another occasion, his guests were discussing this question at table: what renders repose insupportable? The guests debated at great length without any prospect of agreement. The young slave had the audacity to throw in these words: "The feet of a gouty man;" sure of a pardon for his license from the patness of the remark—and the question was solved. On another occasion, pointing to an envious character who appeared that day more gloomy than usual — "Some misfortune, said he, has happened to that man, or some good fortune to someone else."

The master of Syrus desired that a liberal education should grace such rare faculties, and accordingly gave him one. He afterwards added the gift of liberty, a kindness which Syrus never forgot, which substituted for the bonds of servitude, ties dearer to both.

"An affectionate freedman," said Syrus, "is a son acquired without the aid of nature."

At this period of his life it was, that according to the custom of freedmen, he took the name Publius which was doubtless the surname of his master. It has been long maintained by some, but without proof, that he received it much later in life, from the favor of the people.

Hardly had Syrus received his freedom, when he visited Italy, and there gave himself up to the composition of Mimes, a kind of theatrical exhibition at that time very popular. This species of drama must not be confounded with pantomime, in which dancing and gesture represented only a series of disconnected pictures, for Ovid informs us that his *Art of Love* was exhibited in this way nor with the

Greek Mimes, in which the sentiment uttered was of more importance than the performance of the actors. The Mimes of the Romans, from which dancing was gradually banished, consisted at first of burlesque attitudes, and gross and often licentious farces, a species of entertainment more to the taste of the rabble than the regular Greek Mime and better adapted besides to representation in theaters which admitted eighty thousand spectators.

As it was the chief purpose of the Mimes to raise a laugh, they were used to represent the failings and eccentricities of the higher classes, and the vulgar language and solecisms of the lower. Good imitation was therefore their perfection, and they were so pleasing to the Romans that even in funeral processions, a band of mimics performed beside the chief mourners, whose leader imitated the voice and gestures of the deceased.

Emboldened by success, they soon began to act little scenes which had no connection with each other, it is true, but in which the author himself performed the principal part, and in which each of the other actors, who played barefoot, added to his part whatever his own genius might suggest. As there could be no final scene in a play without plot, whenever an actor could not carry out his part, he took to his heels, and his flight put an end to the play.

The mimetic art was in this condition, that is to say, in its infancy, when Syrus composed his mimes. Laberius, a Roman knight, had just produced the first examples of mimetic poetry. Though aiming to amuse the people, he desired to instruct them, and therefore sought to blend useful truths and noble maxims with the pleasantries demanded in this species of comedy. He made the theater a school of morals, and a vehicle of political satire; and although he did not perform in his own pieces from a regard to his rank, he sprinkled them with biting epigrams designed to hit the all-powerful Caesar.

Syrus followed him closely in this new path. He tempered the license of the mimes with many grave features, and a morality so severe, that Seneca, in his disquisitions on the Stoic philosophy, often cited their maxims as authority, and still more frequently made them the themes of lengthy essays.

Syrus traveled Italy for a long time, writing and playing by turns, everywhere applauded as a poet and as an actor. The fame of his success finally reached Rome, and an occasion offered for his appearance there with honor to himself. When Caesar was elected dictator a second time, he resolved to give the enslaved Romans such shows and amusements as should surpass in splendor and duration everything they had before seen. Many days were to be devoted to games, to contests of all kinds, to theatrical representations in all quarters of the city, and in all languages of the then known world; conquered kings were to take part in them. To add to the success and splendor of the performances, Caesar had solicited the presence of the most celebrated writers and actors, and among others, called Syrus to Rome. The news of the exhibitions attracted such multitudes from the neighboring provinces, that, as the houses were full, it was necessary to pitch tents for them in the streets and open fields; and many citizens, among them two senators, were crushed to death by the crowd.

Quite proud of his provincial success, when Syrus arrived in Rome, he had the courage to challenge to a trial of wits all the poets who adorned the stage. Every one accepted the challenge, and they were everyone beaten. The caprice of Caesar brought out against him, however, a formidable competitor. The dictator had commanded Laberius, then sixty years of age, to perform in one of his own mimes, which was a disgrace for a freeman, and above all for a knight. Laberius submitted, but his vengeance was at hand. The day and hour of the contest came. Caesar was the judge, and all the senators and magistrates were its spectators, together with the whole order of knights, all the generals of the victorious army, all the strangers whom conquest or curiosity had made the guests of Rome, and last of all the people, that people whose highest desires were now comprised in bread and public shows. Laberius appeared on the stage, and began, in an admirable prologue, with deploring his compulsory appearance, as an actor, so little in keeping with his age and rank.

"Behold me, then, who after having spent a life of sixty years without a stain on my honor, have left my house a knight, to return to it a mere actor. I have lived too long by one day."

Then thinking of the talent of his young rival, and fearing a defeat, he added, to extenuate its possible disgrace, and gain the pity of the spectators — "What do I bring upon the stage to day? I have lost everything — beauty of form, grace of mien, energy of expression, and the advantage of a good utterance. Like a tomb, I bear on my person only a name."

But he soon recovered his self-possession, and in his performance launched against tyranny a torrent of severe invective, the application of which was readily seen. Thus acting the part of a slave, escaping from the hands of his executioner, he fled shouting — "It is all over with us, Romans, liberty is lost!"

"He who becomes a terror to multitudes," he added a moment after, "has multitudes to dread" — while his gaze was continually fixed on the impassible dictator.

The performance ended, Caesar invited the audacious actor to take a seat among the spectators of his own rank. Syrus, whose turn to perform had now come, then approaching Laberius, said with a modest air, "Please be so good as to receive with kindness as a spectator, him against whom you have contended as an actor."

Laberius sought a place among the ranks of the knights, who however crowded together so as not to allow him a seat. Cicero, who was somewhat given to raillery, shouted to him from a distance, directing his irony at once against the actor and the new batch of senators: "I would cheerfully give you my place, if it were not too much crowded."

"I am astonished," pertly replied Laberius, "to hear that from a man who is wont to sit so well on two seats at once;" a witty allusion to the equivocal character of the orator, a friend at the same time of Caesar and Pompey. He seated himself as he best could, to listen to his rival.

Syrus at length appeared, the crowd shouting their applause, and played the piece he had composed; but we are ignorant even of its title. Whether from resentment, or a sense of justice, Caesar awarding to Syrus the prize of the theatrical contest, immediately passed him the triumphal palm, saying to the knight, with a mocking smile, "Although I was on your side, Laberius, a Syrian has beaten you."

"Such is the fate of man," answered the poet; "today, everything; tomorrow, nothing."

Notwithstanding, to restore the honor of the knight, lost by compliance with his own orders, Caesar passed him a gold ring, the symbol of knightly rank, and added to it a generous present of five hundred thousand sesterces.

This solemn contest between the two, greatest mime writers of Rome, was not the last; it was sometimes repeated. But Laberius, thenceforward confessing the superiority of his conqueror, was content with saying, that another would some day claim it over him; while Caesar, according to Aulus Oellius, continued to prefer Syrus. After the death of his rival, and notwithstanding his jealous predictions, Syrus reigned sole master of the stage for nearly fifteen years, and he continued sole master of it during the rest of his life, which was prolonged, as is generally supposed, to the beginning of the reign of Augustus in 29 BC.

Many testimonials of the ancients prove that the renown of this writer did by no means die with him, and St. Jerome informs us, that after the lapse of four centuries, he was read by the Roman youth in the public schools. Seneca, the tragedian, borrowed from him more than once, and the philosopher often speaks in his praise.

"He is," said he, "the most sublime of dramatic poets, when he abstains from the nothings designed for the lowest benches of the amphitheater."

"How well, he writes on another occasion, would his sayings become, not the barefooted actors of mimes, but the buskined tragedian!"

Macrobius and Aulus Gellius, who with Seneca have done most to preserve us these sayings, are as loud in their praises of them as the philosopher. Petronius, who admired this author so much as to compare him with Cicero, grants the latter superiority in acquirements only: "Syrus," said he, "had the nobler soul."

THE SAYINGS

1. As men, we are all equal in the presence of death.
2. The evil you do to others you may expect in return.
3. Allay the anger of your friend by kindness.
4. To dispute with a drunkard is to debate with an empty house.
5. Receive an injury rather than do one.
6. A trifling rumor may cause a great calamity.
7. To do two things at once is to do neither.
8. A hasty judgment is a first step to a recantation.
9. Suspicion cleaves to the dark side of things.
10. To love one's wife with too much passion, is to be an adulterer.

11. Hard is it to correct the habit already formed.

12. A small loan makes a debtor; a great one, an enemy.

13. Age conceals the lascivious character; age also reveals it.

14. Bitter for a free man is the bondage of debt.

15. Even when we get what we wish, it is not ours.

16. We are interested in others, when they are interested in us.

17. Every one excels in something in which another fails.

18. Do not find your happiness in another's sorrow.

19. An angry lover tells himself many lies.

20. A lover, like a torch, burns the more fiercely the more agitated.

21. Lovers know what they want, but not what they need.

22. A lover's suspicions are a waking man's dreams.

23. There is no penalty attached to a lover's oath.

24. The anger of lovers renews the strength of love.

25. A god could hardly love and be wise.

26. Love is youth's privilege, but an old man's shame.

27. If your parent is just, revere him; if not, bear with him.

28. If you cannot bear the faults of a friend, you make them your own [because you have not the charity to correct them].

29. Be not blind to a friend's faults, nor hate him for them.

30. If you bear the faults of a friend, you make them your own [that is, you show a disposition to correct them].

31. When you fall short in what is due to yourself, you are lacking towards your friends.

32. Friendship either finds or makes equals.

33. Friendship ever profits, but love ever injures.

34. Confidence is the only bond of friendship.

35. Adversity shows whether we have friends, or only the shadows of friends.

36. We should not injure a friend even in sport.

37. The loss of a friend is the greatest of losses.

38. The loss which is unknown is no loss at all.

39. Love cannot be stifled, but it may die out.

40. There can be no alliance between Love and Fear.

41. Love is the source of an idle anxiety.

42. Love; like a tear, rises in the eye and falls upon the breast.

43. Time, not the will, can put an end to love.

44. Love's wounds are cured by their cause.

45. The will controls the beginnings of love, but not its endings.
46. We all seek to know whether we shall be rich; but no one asks whether he shall be good.
47. The plainer the table, the more wholesome the food.
48. We should not credit the utterances of an angry spirit.
49. A wise man rules his passions, a fool obeys them.
50. When reason rules, money is a blessing.
51. Reason guides, and not the eye, when chaste women select; husband.
52. A [haughty] spirit in disgrace is a show for the rabble.
53. Human reason grows rich by self-conquest.
54. To know when to fear, is to be in the path of safety.
55. He has existed only, not lived, who lacks wisdom in old age.
56. Death laughs when old women frolic.
57. Woman becomes good, when she is openly wicked.
58. When the tree has fallen, anyone can cut wood.
59. Tension weakens the bow; the want of it the mind.
60. Art avails nothing, when chance determines the issue.
61. Keep a sharp watch where you would not lose.
62. Excessive severity misses its own aim.
63. Audacity augments courage; hesitation, fear.
64. If you cannot become a harper, become a piper.
65. When Gold argues the cause, eloquence is impotent.
66. Woman loves or hates: she knows no middle course.
67. Concert of action renders slight aid efficient.
68. What greater evil could you wish a miser, than long life?
69. You can easily get the better of Avarice, if you are not avaricious yourself.
70. Money does not sate Avarice, but stimulates it.
71. No amount of gain satisfies Avarice.
72. The [rich] miser suffers more from a loss than a [poor] sage.
73. Avarice is the source of its own sorrows.
74. The avaricious man's best deed is his death.
75. Greediness ill-becomes any one; least of all; an old man.
76. A well-planned project often turns out ill.
77. He sleeps well; who knows not that he sleeps ill.
78. It is well to yield up a pleasure; when a pain goes with it.

79. The guilty man deserves to lose the money with which he would bribe the judge.

80. Happy he who died when death was desirable.

81. A good reputation is a second patrimony.

82. We make the nearest approaches to the gods in our good deeds.

83. No one but a knave or a fool thinks a good deed thrown away.

84. The more benefits bestowed; the more received.

85. Never forget a favor received; be quick to forget a favor bestowed.

86. Gratitude is a spur for your benefactors.

87. To receive a favor is to pawn your freedom.

88. He who cannot give; should not receive.

89. To give to the deserving is to lay all men under obligation.

90. A gift in season is a double favor to the needy.

91. He who boasts of a favor bestowed would like it back again.

92. Sympathy in benevolence is the closest of all kinships.

93. A true benevolence knows the reason of its gifts.

94. To die by another's command is to endure two deaths.

95. A favor granted before it is asked; is doubly acceptable.

96. Past happiness augments present wretchedness.

97. He dies twice who perishes by his own hand.

98. Aid rendered the wrong-doer, makes you the greater sinner.

99. Conquest over one's self; in the hour of victory, is a double triumph.

100. Multiply your acts of kindness and you teach the recipient to return them.

101. Venus yields to caresses, not to compulsion.

102. Mercy shown [to the wretched] may become a bulwark of defense.

103. Happy is the voyage that brings the good together.

104. A good reputation; even in darkness, keeps on shining.

105. A death that ends the [incurable] ills of life, is a blessing.

106. Money is worth something when good sense disburses it.

107. One man's happy hour is another's bitter time of trial.

108. A good reputation is more valuable than money.

109. We must master our good fortune, or it will master us.

110. It is a happy disgrace that saves from a greater peril.

111. The slothful enjoyment of it, is the worst part of prosperity.

112. Even in death, a good man would not deceive.
113. To spare the guilty is to injure the innocent.
114. The more skillfully the language of goodness is assumed the greater the depravity.
115. A good man's severity is next neighbor to justice.
116. A mean man's generosity is a generous man's meanness.
117. A good man loves to sit at a good man's table.
118. In the presence of a good man anger is speedily cooled.
119. It is well to moor your bark with two anchors.
120. Learn to see in another's calamity the ills which you should avoid.
121. The good which is prevented is not annihilated.
122. The slower to kindle; the more terrible the wrath of a generous soul.
123. The good man never coquets with iniquity.
124. Life is short; but its ills make it seem long.
125. The bare recollection of anger kindles anger.
126. There is no sight in the eye when the mind does not gaze.
127. While teasing for horns; the camel lost his ears.
128. He keeps furthest from danger who looks out while he is safe.
129. A chaste wife rules her husband by deferring to his wishes.
130. Misfortune sometimes visits him whom she has often passed by.
131. Trust no man as a friend till you have tried him.
132. Beware of him who has once deceived you.
133. You can never dispense with prudence.
134. The wounds of conscience always leave a scar.
135. The danger despised is the first to reach us.
136. Falsities are quick to appear in their true character.
137. We are anxious to avoid the faults which we are ashamed to have committed.
138. There is but a step between a proud man's glory and his disgrace.
139. The joys of the worthless speedily turn to their own destruction.
140. Oblivion is a guaranty against civil war.
141. Make your beloved angry if you wish him to love you.
142. The request of a master is a command.
143. An agreeable companion on a journey is as good as a carriage.
144. Society in shipwreck is a comfort to all.
145. Congeniality of disposition is the strongest of ties.

146. Consult your conscience; rather than popular opinion.

147. Consider what you ought to say, and not what you think.

148. You will gain your point better by moderation than anger.

149. Many receive advice; few profit by it.

150. We tolerate without rebuke the vices with which we have grown familiar.

151. Man's most prudent counselor is time.

152. Wisdom had rather be buffeted than not be listened to.

153. Folly had rather be unheard than be buffeted.

154. It is hard to touch that which brings pain by mere contact.

155. A god can hardly disturb a man truly happy.

156. Have courage; or cunning; when you deal with an enemy.

157. It is folly to be too frank with impudent familiarity.

158. Let fly many arrows; and no two will hit in the same place.

159. He who longs for death; confesses that life is a failure.

160. The sick man's intemperance makes the physician relentless.

161. Reproach in misfortune is an unseasonable cruelty.

162. It is barbarity; not courage that can slay babes.

163. Tears gratify a savage nature they do not melt it.

164. Anger blazes forth but once against its object.

165. He who has no home is a dead man without a sepulcher.

166. He whom the popular voice approves holds the key of the people's treasure.

167. He who can get more than belongs to him, is apt to accommodate his desires to his opportunity.

168. To be always giving; is to encourage a forcible taking when you refuse to give.

169. Every man is a master in his own calling.

170. Patience is a remedy for every sorrow.

171. What happens to one man may happen to all.

172. When the people detest a man's life; they call for his death.

173. The greatest of comforts is to be free from blame.

174. There is no safety in gaining the favor of an enemy.

175. Anger and inordinate desire are the worst of counselors.

176. To refuse when extreme necessity prays, is to condemn to death.

177. The tongue of the condemned can speak, but cannot avert the doom.

178. The gain acquired at the expense of reputation, should be counted a loss.

179. There is rarely a loss where plenty is unknown.

180. The blessing which could be received, can be taken away.

181. It is enough to think ill of an enemy, without speaking it.

182. You can find more friends at the tenth hour, than at the first.

183. A homely woman is one of the most comely of apes.

184. Wisdom is acquired by meditation.

185. While we stop to think, we often miss our opportunity.

186. Deliberation should be protracted, when the decision is to be final.

187. When utility is our aim, a little delay is advisable.

188. It is madness to put confidence in error.

189. When Providence favors; you can make a safe voyage on a twig.

190. The gods methinks must laugh when a prosperous man puts up a prayer [for more].

191. Whatever you can lose, you should reckon of no account.

192. It is easy for women to shed tears without salt.

193. One day treats us like a hireling nurse, another, like a mother.

194. Fear lest a day snatch away what a single day has acquired.

195. It is hard to keep that which everyone covets.

196. Turn a deaf ear to calumnious reports.

197. Yesterday should be the teacher of today.

198. Discord gives a relish for concord.

199. Reflect on everything you hear, but believe only on proof.

200. Preparations for war should be long in making, that victory may be the more speedy.

201. Divide the fire, and you will the sooner put it out.

202. Mental pain is harder to bear than corporeal.

203. When pain cannot increase, it dies away.

204. He who has prospered in life; should stay at home.

205. The builder of a house should not leave it unfinished.

206. The courage of the soldiers depends upon the wisdom of the general.

207. Avoid the sweet which is like to become a bitter.

208. The rewards of talent and fortune are offered to all.

209. Pleasant is the remembrance of the ills that are past.

210. When life passes agreeably is the best time to die.

211. The more promptly bestowed the greater the kindness.

212. Avoid cupidity, and you conquer a kingdom.

213. The less a mortal desires, the less he needs.

214. How sad his fate, who grows old through anxiety.

216. A kindness should be received in the spirit that prompted it.

216. There is no need of spurs when the horse is running away.

217. In place of giving an angry man arms, we should take them away.

218. Speed itself is slow when cupidity waits.

219. For him who loves labor, there is always something to do.

220. It is a kingly spirit that can return good deeds for reproaches.

221. An inglorious life is the next thing to death.

222. Solitude is the mother of anxieties.

223. The party to which the rabble belong is ever the worst.

224. Even calamity becomes virtue's opportunity.

225. The wretched reflect either too much or too little.

226. Patience is affliction's haven.

227. The good to which we have become accustomed; is often an evil.

228. Even a single hair casts its shadow.

229. Celerity is tardiness when ardent desire urges.

230. He who takes counsel of good faith, is just even to an enemy.

231. We should keep our word even to the undeserving.

232. Pain will force even the truthful to speak falsely.

233. It is sometimes expedient to forget who we are.

234. We may with advantage at times forget what we know.

235. Those who do injustice, hate it.

236. Even when the wound is healed, the scar remains.

237. Even when there is no law, there is conscience.

238. The tyrant can hardly be said to hold even a doubtful sway.

239. Pecuniary gain first suggested to men to make Fortune a god-

240. The fiercer the contention, the more honorable the reconciliation.

241. The hope of reward is the solace of labor.

242. The wise man corrects his own errors by observing those of others.

243. The further the fall, the greater the hurt.

244. Depravity is revealed in outward action, but its source is within.

245. The life which we live is but a small part of the real life.

246. A great man may commence life in a hovel.

247. He suffers exile who refuses to serve his country.

248. Men will judge your past deeds by your last.

249. Versatility of mind is a natural bias to folly.

250. It is easier to add to a great reputation than to get it.

251. Good fortune renders a man agreeable if the good fortune is not seen.

252. By concealing the deed you render the accusation more serious.

253. Calumny is a malevolent lie.

254. Many consult their reputation; but few their conscience.

255. The master is a slave when he fears those whom he rules.

256. He confesses his crime who flees the tribunal.

257. Prosperity is the nurse of ill temper.

258. A prosperous worthlessness is the curse of high life.

259. Endure the heavy burdens, and you will the more easily carry the lighter.

260. Bear without murmuring what cannot be changed.

261. Be patient under your afflictions; that you may be able to endure your happiness.

262. You should hammer your iron when it is glowing hot.

263. No one ever lost honor but him who never had any.

264. He who has forfeited his honor can lose nothing more.

265. What is left when honor is lost?

266. Confidence; like life; never returns to him whom she has once left.

267. A fair exterior is a silent recommendation.

268. Fortune has no lawful control over men's morals.

269. A great property is a great bondage for the owner.

270. Fortune often spares men a present affliction, that they may suffer a greater.

271. Fortune makes a fool of him whom she favors too much.

272. Fortune masters us if we do not master her.

273. Fortune has no more power over our destiny than our own actions.

274. Fortune is not satisfied with inflicting one calamity.

275. When Fortune is on our side, popular favor bears her company.

276. Fortune has more power over a man than his own forethought.

277. When fortune flatters she does it to betray.

278. When the edifice of our Fortune is but slightly fractured; a chasm opens through the whole.

279. Fortune makes many loans but gives no presents.

280. Fortune is like glass; the brighter the glitter the more easily broken.

281. The great gifts of Fortune are waited on by fear.

282. It is more easy to get a favor from Fortune than to keep it.

283. His own character is the arbiter of every one's fortune.

284. It is a fraud to receive the trust which you cannot return.

285. Put a bridle on your tongue but at all hazards on your baser members.

286. With but few; is a repetition of punishment remedial.

287. Frugality is poverty disguised with a good name.

288. Vain are his prayers who cannot grant a prayer.

289. An over-taxed patience gives way to fierce anger.

290. The future struggles that it may not become the past

291. Where there is no shame there is double the guilt

292. Groans show the pain but do not remove it.

293. A noble steed is not annoyed by the barking of dogs.

294. The gladiator lays his plans after he enters the arena.

295. The termination of a present is one step toward a future evil.

296. It vexes a cheerful giver to meet with a scowling acceptance.

297. A serious charge; even when mildly uttered; gives pain.

298. It is a grave accusation which admits of no defense.

299. It is a useless defense which cannot find a fair trial.

300. The most formidable enemy lies hid in one's own heart.

301. There are some remedies worse than the disease.

302. Prudent minds come to settled conclusions.

303. Repentance for our past deeds is a severe mental punishment.

304. The anger of the righteous man is the anger most to be dreaded.

305. Powerful indeed is the empire of habit.

306. The evil that visits us with a smiling countenance; is the hardest to bear.

307. The severest auction is the one which has never been tried.

308. Frequent marriages give occasion to slander.

309. A flattering discourse carries its own poison.

310. Do not take part in the council; unless you are called.

311. He who stops in mid-career is not quite lost.

312. Better endure an heir, than seek for one.

313. Under the tears of an heir, there is hidden a smile.

314. How difficult is it to keep the glory acquired!

315. How formidable is he who has no fear of death!

316. Circumstances will oft force a good man to swerve from the right.

317. Poverty compels men to many untried expedients.

318. By doing nothing men learn to do ill.

319. Amid a multitude of projects no plan is devised.

320. When angry a man has deserted his body.

321. Men made Fortune a goddess, that misfortune might be certain.

322. It is easy for men to say one thing, and think another.

323. We die, as often as we lose a friend.

324. Man's life is a loan, not a gift.

325. Necessity is a law that justifies itself.

326. Success makes some crimes honorable.

327. An honorable death is better than a disgraceful life.

328. Honors are soiled when they invest the unworthy.

329. The well-born should not live base lives.

330. It is right to spare the guilty, when you thereby shield the innocent.

331. To submit to necessity involves no disgrace.

332. Honors adorn the worthy; they are a stigma to the undeserving.

333. That is the noblest emulation which humanity prompts.

334. Humility neither falls far nor heavily.

335. The people are strongest, where the Laws have most power.

336. Victory waits upon unity of action.

337. When the world hates you; see that it have no good therefor.

338. When two do the same thing; it is not the same thing after all.

339. Indolence never lacks excuse to avoid labor.

340. A fire can be seen at a great distance when it gives no heat.

341. Gold is tried by fire, fortitude by affliction.

342. It is humane to forgive when the forgiven blushes at the kindness.

343. Pardon the offense of others, but never your own.

344. The sinner's judgment began the day that he sinned.

345. Would you have a great empire? Rule over yourself.

346. The sinner who repented after the offense, was a little imprudent

347. It is not wrong to harm him, who has done wrong to you.
348. Authority has less influence than beauty; where love is concerned.
349. When we yield to love, we are aiding to our own haven.
350. Love's anger is always hypocritical.
351. A laugh at the unfortunate is a wrong done him.
352. Committed against the unfortunate injustice is powerful.
353. Life itself is an insult to the wretched.
354. That life is most pleasant which is passed in ignorance.
355. Avarice is kind to no one; and most cruel toward itself.
356. Audacity is every things when the danger is critical.
357. A cock has great influence on his own dung-hill.
358. Anyone can hold the helm, when the sea is calm.
359. When the offense is a disgrace, it is a double sin to commit it.
360. Pain and pleasure vie with each other in love.
361. The madness of love is ever delightful.
362. Haste is a crime, when the judge is deliberating.
363. To be not too sanguine of our conclusions, is one half of wisdoms.
364. Indolence consists in seeking excuses from labor.
365. When labor is shunned, laziness shows its face.
366. Innocence is the solace of the wretched.
367. The subordinate perceives all the failings of his superior.
368. It is a weak mind that cannot bear the possession of riches.
369. A truly noble nature cannot be insulted.
370. To request an unworthy action offends a manly spirit.
371. A noble soul has no fear for unjust reproaches.
372. Those are unacceptable favors that carry terror to the recipient.
373. Earth produces no viler creature than an ingrate.
374. One ingrate is a curse to the whole world of unfortunates.
375. No prayers reach the heart of an enemy.
376. No tears are shed when an enemy dies.
377. However humble your enemy it is wise to fear him.
378. To avenge one's self on an enemy, is to receive a second life.
379. A neighbor is apt to look on our affairs with an evil eye.
380. Slander is more injurious than open violence.
381. The ear bears an injury better than the eye.
382. It is easier to do an injury than to bear one.

383. To forget the wrongs you receive, is to remedy them.
384. He confers a double favor on the needy, who gives in season.
385. Poverty needs little; avarice everything.
386. The madman thinks the rest of the world crazy.
387. Cupidity in the midst of riches is an armed indigence.
388. The bow too tensely strung is easily broken.
389. To do good you should know what good is.
390. There is more venom than truth in the words of envy.
391. The rancor of envy is concealed, but is none the less hostile.
392. To withstand the assaults of envy, you must be either a hero or a saint.
393. It is more agreeable to be envied than pitied.
394. Crimes are encouraged by overlooking petty offenses.
395. Detain a man against his will, and you urge him to depart.
396. Shun an angry man for a moment —your enemy forever.
397. Anger thinks crime justifiable.
398. Every word of an angry man conveys a reproach.
399. When the angry man grows cool, he is angry with himself.
400. That mortal needs least; who wishes least.
401. Treat your friend as if he might become an enemy.
402. Put such confidence in your friend, that he shall find no cause to become an enemy.
403. Where one has led the way, another may follow.
404. Every excellence continues unknown, which fame does not call abroad.
405. Pleasant to see, is the stain from the blood of an enemy.
406. No pleasure endures unseasoned by variety.
407. The judge is condemned, when the criminal is acquitted.
408. The right is ever beyond the reach of the wrong
409. The magistrate should hear both right and wrong side.
410. The gods give man one good; as an offset to two ills.
411. Labor is the best of condiments for youth's food.
412. When injured, our enemy's anguish assuages our own.
413. The error repeated is a fault.
414. Libertinage and moral worth never go together.
415. When you bestow favors on a multitude, many will be thrown away for a single one that goes to the right place.
416. When vice is approved, it will soon become intolerable.

417. Unless a man adds to his glory, he loses what he has.

418. The guilty dread the law, the innocent fear fortune.

419. Anger is apt to forget the existence of law.

420. Hares can gambol over the body of a dead lion.

421. It is a universal law which ordains birth and death.

422. Caprice is the mark of a frivolous spirit.

423. Frivolity; not sobriety, affects intemperate enjoyment.

424. The Law keeps her eye on the angry man, when he does not see the Law.

425. When the lion is dead, even puppies can bite him.

426. He who chases two hares will catch neither.

427. Fortune is fickle, and speedily asks back her favors.

428. The love of pleasure is universal, though every face does not show it.

429. When you assail truth, you may give loose reins to your tongue.

430. Dignities heaped on the undeserving, are a badge of disgrace.

431. A slanderous tongue is the sign of a bad heart.

432. He who lives in solitude, may make his own laws.

433. A long life makes acquaintance with a thousand ills.

434. Far distant seems the object when desire is ardent

435. Profits in trade can be made only by another's loss.

436. Nature finds us better heirs than our testaments.

437. The greater our strength, the less we know of the power of misfortune.

438. In the art of praying, necessity is the best of teachers.

439. Practice is the best of all instructors.

440. A great fortune sits gracefully on a great man.

441. A noble spirit finds a cure for injustice in forgetting it.

442. Mighty rivers may easily be leaped at their source.

443. Excessive indignation is sometimes evidence of a great crime.

444. It is a bad cause that takes refuge in the lenity of the judge.

445. Hard to bear is the poverty which follows [a bad use of] riches.

446. It is a bad medicine that exhausts the powers of nature.

447. It is a sorry pleasure which is dispensed at the pleasure of another.

448. A miserable death is an insult from destiny.

449. Dispositions naturally bad have little need of a teacher.

450. When you merely wish for what is disgraceful, you violate decorum.

451. It is bad management when we suffer fortune to be our guide.

452. The physician were ill; if no one else were ill.

453. Supreme power may be lost by an abuse of power.

454. The patient treats his case badly when he makes the physician his heir.

455. He must have lived ill who knows not how to die well.

456. By showing how an evil can be done, you make it worse.

457. They live ill who expect to live always.

458. Malevolence keeps its teeth hidden.

459. He who is bent on doing evil, can never want occasion.

460. An envious disposition feeds upon itself.

461. It is a sad victory which brings repentance in the hour of triumph.

462. The ungrateful above all others, teach us severity and distrust

463. One man's wickedness may easily become all men's curse.

464. Depravity pretends to goodness, that it may be worse than before.

465. You may spare a bad man if a good one must die with him.

466. Woman is man's superior in cunning.

467. Never find your delight in another's misfortune.

468. Evil counsels are the greatest curse to him who gives them.

469. It is a bad plan that admits of no modification.

470. He is a bad servant who teaches his master.

471. The more reconciled the worse the thoughts of a bad heart.

472. An evil mind cannot counsel well for itself.

473. The vicious are most to be feared, when they pretend to be good.

474. He should be called bad, who is good only for selfish ends.

476. When the ill-declined cannot do mischief, they still dream of it.

476. He will become wicked himself, who feasts with the wicked.

477. In the punishment of the wicked, there is safety for the good.

478. When the case is clear, it pronounces judgment for itself.

479. A gentle course is a safe one, but it invites oppression.

480. When you are at sea, keep clear of the land.

481. Equanimity is calamity's medicine.

482. Oblivion is the only remedy for wretchedness.

483. Intemperance is the physician's provider.

484. It is better to have a little than nothing.
485. A mistress is an occasion of dishonor.
486. Fear cannot restrain, when pleasure invites.
487. Fear old age, for it does not come without company.
488. That must be always guarded, which you would keep safely.
489. Fear, and not kindness, restrains the vicious.
490. There is poor sleeping with care for a bedfellow.
491. The less Fortune has given, the less can she take away.
492. The prompter the refusal, the less the disappointment.
493. The master who fears his slave, is the greater slave.
494. The good man can be called miserable, but he is not so.
495. Wretched the pleasure which is alloyed with a sense of panic.
496. Unhappy he who most pass life in the midst of perils.
497. To live free from danger is to know nothing of misery.
498. A beneficent citizen is a blessing to his country.
499. It is an unhappy lot which finds no enemies.
500. It is an unhappy lot which an enemy does not envy.
501. To depend on another's nod for a livelihood is a sad destiny.
502. Compulsory silence is intolerable when one burns to speak freely.
503. Methinks you are unhappy, if you never have been so.
504. There is diligence in mature deliberation.
505. Delay is always vexatious, but it is wisdom's opportunity.
506. Understand your friend's character, but do not hate it.
507. An orator's life is more convincing than his eloquence.
508. Happy the man who dies before he prays for death.
509. You must die, but not as often as you may have wished.
510. There is no mortal whom sorrow cannot reach.
511. The fear of death is more to be dreaded than death itself.
512. When you have learned to despise death, you will have over-come every terror.
513. Everything which has birth, must pay tribute to death.
514. A woman's tear is spite's seasoning.
515. There are many displeased when a woman weds many.
516. A woman's solitary thoughts are her worst ones.
517. You will find a great many things before you find a good man.
518. Power gains power by a multitude of pardons.
519. He threatens many, who does injustice to one.

520. Seek to please many, and you seek a failure.

521. The death of a good man is a public calamity.

522. He whom many fear, has himself many to fear.

523. Gifts, and not tears, soften the heart of a courtesan.

524. A rolling stone gathers no moss.

525. When her anger is kindled by injustice; goodness changes her norm.

526. When a vile man does right he conceals his true character.

527. Let not your benevolence extend beyond your means.

528. Never promise more than you can perform.

529. Begin nothings the accomplishment of which you will repent.

530. No one can escape death or love.

531. Man has no enduring lease of life or fortune.

532. Necessity may force from men whatever she wishes.

533. Necessity imposes laws; but does not receive them.

534. Want renders a needy man a liar.

535. On what a firm foundation rests the empire of necessity.

536. In vain may we look for that which fate conceals.

537. Necessity takes what she wishes by force if not voluntarily yielded.

538. We should bear our destiny, not weep over it.

539. Necessity can turn any weapon to advantage.

540. A wise man never refuses anything to necessity.

541. Frugality is a remedy for indigence.

542. Avarice never lacks a reason for refusing a favor.

543. We refuse ourselves [the thing desired], when we ask what cannot be had.

544. It is natural not to credit [the possibility of] great crimes.

545. No one should be judge in his own cause.

546. No one dies too soon, whom misery slays.

547. No one is so poor during life, as at birth.

548. Be the first to laugh at your own blunder, and no one will laugh at you.

549. Fear never advanced any man to the highest standing.

550. Depravity is its own greatest punishment.

551. When the bad imitate the good, there is no knowing what mischief is intended.

552. He who is always unlucky, had better do nothing.

553. Necessity knows no law except to conquer.

554. Fortune takes nothing away but her own gifts.

555. There is nothing more wretched than a mind conscious of its own wickedness.

556. Our most poignant reflections arise from shame for past acts.

557. Nothing can be done at once hastily and prudently.

558. It is pleasant to do a favor for him who does not ask it.

559. We desire nothing so much as what we ought not to have.

560. There is nothing which the lapse of time will not either extinguish or improve.

561. There is no fruit which is not bitter before it is ripe.

562. The eyes are not responsible when the mind does the seeing.

563. To be deprived of all capacity for action, is to be at once alive and dead.

564. Consider nothing which is liable to change a permanent possession.

565. Consider nothing beneath your notice which may contribute to your safety.

566. There is no more shameful sight, than an old man commencing life.

567. Too much candor is easily duped.

568. The truth is lost when there is too much contention about it

569. If there is no evil in death, there is too much good in it.

570. Stretch the cord too tightly, and it will be likely to break.

571. It is only the ignorant who despise education.

572. It is vain to be the pupil of a sage if you have no brains yourself.

573. He can best avoid a snare who knows how to set one.

574. Not to punish offenses, is to encourage depravity.

575. Guilty men beg, the innocent are indignant.

576. The ready apologist of guilt may be himself suspected.

577. A resolute spirit is not cast down by a single misfortune.

578. To abstain from doing injury when you have the power to do it, deserves the greatest praise.

579. Do not despise the lowest steps in the ascent to greatness.

580. Don't turn back when you are just at the goal.

581. It is not every question that deserves an answer.

582. He is not likely to perish in the ruins who trembles at a crack in the wall.

583. To control a man against his will is not to correct him, but injure him.

584. No man is happy who does not think himself so.

585. It is not goodness to be barely better than the worst are.

586. No scar is dishonorable which is a mark of our courage.

587. There can never be an surplus of honorable actions.

588. The anguish thoroughly allayed should not be rudely awakened.

589. That is not very small which is barely less than the greatest.

590. That is not yours which fortune made yours.

591. It is hard to think the habitually innocent guilty of crime.

592 You will find it difficult to be sole guardian over that which multitudes covet.

593. Never thrust your own sickle into another's corn.

594. A prompt refusal is sometimes no slight service.

595. Courage cannot be cast down by adversity.

596. You cannot put the same shoe on every foot.

597. Do not suppose everything will come to pass as you have arranged for it.

598. He bids fair to grow wise, who has discovered that he is not so.

599. Don't consider how many you can please, but whom.

600. Good fortune does not always lend a ready ear.

601. It is not safe to indulge in a play of wits with kings.

602. It is never too late to take the road to rectitude.

603. To yield to our friends is not to be overcome but to conquer.

604. There is no pleasure which continued enjoyment cannot render disgusting.

605. Misfortune is most men's greatest punishment.

606. Of all men the bad man's fellow can be most readily found.

607. Never thrust upon another the burden you cannot carry yourself.

608. Pity is well spoken of in all lands.

609. There is no great evil which does not bring with it some advantage.

610. Consider that there is no place without a [hidden] witness.

611 No wise man has ever put faith in a traitor.

612. Our greatest gains are made by sparing what we possess [i.e. by economy].

613. Crimes are most easily concealed in the midst of a crowd.

614. He is never happy whose thoughts always ran with his fears.

615. No danger incurred, no danger repelled.

616. You can never give enough to satisfy unlawful expectations.

617. A guilty conscience never feels secure.

618. Where a fire has long burned there is always some smoke.

619. The worst danger is that which is concealed.

620. Who knows how great are the secret pangs of conscience?

621. How long is life to the wretched; how short for the happy!

622. The kind attentions of the wife speedily gender disgust for the concubine.

623. Opportunities are easily lost with difficulty found.

624. It is hard to recover the lost opportunity.

625. It is an honorable death that delivers from an ignominious servitude.

626. When the performer is concealed, we are indifferent to the music.

627. Put more confidence in your eyes than your ears.

628. I dislike a precocious talent in little boys.

629. He is a despicable sage whose wisdom does not profit himself.

630. Some enmities conceal themselves beneath a mask, some under a kiss.

631. Every vicious act has its excuse ever ready.

632. A cheerful obedience is universal when the worthy bear rule.

633. Every day should be passed as if it were to be our last.

634. Every fascinating pleasure is an injurious pleasure.

635. There should be no disagreement between our lives and our doctrines.

636. Be at war with men's vices, at peace with themselves.

637. Crafty and not sorrow, is seen in a hypocrite's tears.

638. An angry father is most cruel toward himself.

639. To know how to obey is as honorable as to role.

640. Familiarity breeds contempt.

641. Easy is the intercourse of equals with equals.

642. We find something of the favor sought in a graceful refusal.

643. A prompt denial is something toward the favor requested.

644. Hunger goes with stinted supplies, disgust attends on abundance.

645. By tolerating many abuses, we encourage the assaults of such as we cannot tolerate.

646. Patience and fortitude create their own happiness.

647. Patience in adversity is by no means felicity.

648. Patience reveals the soul's hidden riches.

649. Any land is your country where you can live happy.

650. There are few to appreciate what God gives to all.

651. A few men's depravity is all men's calamity.

652. There are few unwilling to sin, none without knowledge thereof.

653. It is right to wish your friend's fault concealed.

654. You do well to consider your friend's error your own.

665. He who promptly corrects, makes his error the less.

656. Money alone sets all the world in motion.

657. Be your money's master, not its slave.

658. The worse the precepts, the more easy for youth to learn.

659. Mute grief feels a keener pang than that which cries aloud.

660. Always study to secure your permanent peace.

661. An end to our gettings is the only end to our losses.

662. The greater will be lost; if the less is not saved.

663. A gift is a loss; where gratitude is not the receiver.

664. It is the soul; not the body, that makes an enduring marriage.

665. To know the hour of death is to die every moment.

666. A happy man is he who obtains his wishes easily.

667. To take refuge with an inferior is to betray one's self.

668. The timid man sees dangers that do not exist.

669. He who dares danger, triumphs over it before it reaches him.

670. He who exercises clemency gains a victory for all time.

671. No one can long sustain a false character.

672. He invites danger who indulges in anger.

673. He who has plenty of pepper, will pepper his cabbage.

674. You should go to a pear tree for pears, not to an elm.

675. It is a very hard undertaking to seek to please everybody.

676. Friends delight in the dishes which cordiality seasons.

677. Most men are good through fear, not through a love of goodness.

678. God generally finds a way for like to meet like.

679. Fortune shields more people than she secures.

680. Harken rather to your conscience than to opinion.

681. It is easier to submit to punishment than to injustice.

682. To live in misery and destitution is worse than punishment

683. Slander is a greater outrage than personal violence.

684. Punishment creeps upon wickedness secretly in order to crush it.

685. The less the pain, the lighter the punishment.

686. Punishment tarries for vice, but never passes it by.

687. Whoever is useful to his country, is the people's property.

688. The memory of great misfortunes suffered, is itself a misfortune.

689. A merciful man in power is a public blessing.

690. To get angry with power, is to invite danger on one's own head.

691. Freedom alone is the source of noble action.

692. Prosperity has no power over adversity.

693. He whose vengeance is sated in his absence, is ever present with his victim.

694. Methinks it is better to be envied than pitied.

695. It is deception to refuse first, and afterward perform.

696. Gratitude for a favor is sufficient interest therefor.

697. To do wrong for a master is a meritorious act.

698. The pain which kills pain, is as good as a medicine.

699. When you have good materials, employ good workmen.

700. The judge who ignores a good man's offenses, wipes them out.

701. A good reputation is a good man's noblest inheritance.

702. He who does a kindness to the deserving, shares it with him.

703. A worthy freedman is a son acquired without the aid of nature.

704. Unhappy he, who cannot do the good that he would.

705. He benefits who will not injure when he can.

706. It is an unjust sentence which extends the deserved penalty too far.

707. He who is eager to condemn, takes delight in condemning.

708. A hasty verdict betrays a desire to find a crime committed.

709. We should provide in peace what we need in war.

710. Wit itself is folly in a sage.

711. Lost modesty never returns to grace the loser.

712. Modesty may be born, it never can be taught.

713. He will yield to fear, who has no regard for honor.

714. The nurselings of avarice have but a short time to stay.

715. God looks at the clean hands, not the full ones.

716. You need not seek twice for the rose already withered.

717. In being modest there is a slight touch of servility.

718. He who violates another's honor loses his own.

719. The friendship that can come to an end, never really began.

720. What it is right to do, should be done at the right time.

721. Do not seek for that which you would be ashamed to find.

722. The woman too anxious to seem fair, cannot say No.

723. Look for a tough wedge for a tough log.

724. How oppressive is the weight of an evil conscience!

725. How happy the life unembarassed by the cares of business!

726. How great a matter is it to deserve praise, though we do not receive it!

727. How vile is he who charges his own offenses upon others!

728. How much to be pitied is he, who has no pity!

729. How unhappy is he who cannot forgive himself!

730. How poor the assistance which injures while it aids!

731. How hard it is to be compelled to regret our good deeds!

732. Sad is it to be forced to ruin him whom you would save.

733. It is a great loss to lose that which few possess.

734. Unhappy fate, to long for death and be unable to find it.

735. It is a great grievance when the evil which is past returns again.

736. How hard it is when accident triumphs over design!

737. It is a bitter fate when one's defenders become his jailors.

738. How bootless the kindness which is followed by no good result!

739. How much must he repent of who lives a long life!

740. How often must he ask for pardon who has refused it when asked!

741. How timid is he who stands in terror of poverty!

742. The bitterness of the admonition never does harm.

743. Consider the useful agreeable even though it were not.

744. When our incense falls short, we offer salt cakes.

745. It is wrong even to complain of him whom you love.

746. He whom public opinion has once degraded, rarely recovers his former standing.

747. If you delight in the society of the vicious; you are vicious yourself.

748. He who can best play the hypocrite, can soonest injure his enemy.

749. How shall we treat with those who say one thing, and mean another?

750. Pardon one offense, and you encourage the commission of many more.

751. The debtor does not like the sight of his creditor's door.

752. He who yields a prudent obedience, exercises a partial control.

753. He makes many offenders, who is reluctant to punish.

754. He lessens the favor conferred, who waits to be asked.

765. He is suspected on all matters, who makes a failure in one.

756. He who hesitates to take the right course, deliberates to no purpose.

757. A slave against his will is wretched, but none the less a slave.

758. He who adheres to his oath will come out where he wishes.

759. They who plow the sea do not carry the winds in their hands.

760. He who guards against calamities rarely meets them.

761. It is no vice to keep a vice out of sight.

762. He who can play the fool at pleasure can be wise if he will.

763. He who has the power to injure is feared in his absence.

764. He who has the power to harm is dreaded when he does not intend harm.

765. He who can transfer his love [to a new object] can subdue it.

766. It is the height of eloquence to speak in the defense of the innocent.

767. He gets through too late who goes too fast.

768. He who coaxes after he is hurt is prudent out of time.

769. He who praises himself will speedily find a censor.

770. He who accuses himself rarely wants good reason for it.

771. He who lives only for himself is truly dead to others.

772. He who fears his friend teaches his friend to fear him.

773. He who distrusts his friend knows not the meaning of the word.

774. He who dreads all manner of snares will fall into none.

775. He who comes to injure intended the evil before he set out.

776 Give to the good and a share returns to yourself.

777. In every enterprise consider where you would come out.

778. Virtue's deeds are glory's deeds.

779. The honors for which we are indebted to fortune, quickly lose their luster.

780. It takes a long time to bring excellence to maturity.

781. The highest condition takes its rise in the lowest.

782. He who has learned how to injure, recollects the lesson when occasion offers.

783. You should tell no one what you wish no one to know.

784. What is it to practice benevolence? It is to imitate the Deity.

785. It matters not what you are thought to be, but what you are.

786. No one knows what he can do till he tries.

787. What do you need of money if you cannot use it?

788. The defect which one period of life fastens upon us another will remove.

789. Some men are bitter enemies and poor friends.

790. They pass peaceful lives who ignore mine and thine.

791. Who would recognize the unhappy if grief had no language?

792. Who is a poor man? He who thinks himself rich.

793. Who has the greatest possessions? He who wants least

794. What you blame in others as a fault; you should not be guilty of yourself.

795. Neglect a danger and it will some time take you by surprise.

796. The wise man guards against future evils as if they were present.

797. What it is disgraceful to do; think it no honor to speak of.

798. That which you thought to run away from, will often meet you face to face.

799. It is foolish to hoard; when you know not for whom you do it.

800. It is the height of folly to blame without knowledge.

801. We can lament for that which is lost, but we cannot get it back.

802. What we admire, we never cease commending to ourselves.

803. That does not always please us which is always within reach.

804. The world thinks that old age always speaks wisely.

805. What we fear comes to pass more speedily than what we hope.

806. It matters not with what purpose you do it, if the act itself be bad.

807. That which is hardly brought to pass hardly gives pleasure.

808. Passion dreams of what it desires, not of what, is becoming.

809. He can have what he wishes who wishes just enough.

810. When the soul rules over itself its empire is lasting.

811. Even the Milesians were once valiant.

812. Calamity can easily discover whomsoever she seeks.

813. A man has as many enemies in his own house as he has slaves.

814. He is condemned every day who stands in daily fear of condemnation.

815. The next day is never as good as the day before.

816. When you are in love you are not wise; or, when you are wise you are not in love.

817. When you give to avarice you invite an injury.

818. When you forgive an enemy you gain many friends.

819. When a wise man conquers himself, his conquest is worth something.

820. When vice is profitable, he errs who does right.

821. A frog would leap from a throne of gold into a puddle.

822. It is robbery to receive a favor which you cannot return.

823. It is robbing, not asking, when you take from a man against his will.

824. That must be rare which you desire to be a long time precious.

825. He is truly wise who gains wisdom from another's mishap.

826. Youth should be governed by reason, not by force.

827. Good health and good sense are two of life's greatest blessings.

828. He who gives to each man his due, pays a debt and loses nothing himself.

829. It matters not how long you live but how well.

830. Don't turn back when you are just at the goal.

831. He who imposes his own talk on the circle; does not converse; he plays the master.

832. Fortune tosses off her wheel the destinies of kings.

833. Delay profits nothing but a hasty temper.

834. We get rid of bitter bile with bitter medicines.

835. It is vain to look for a defense against lightning.

836. It is more tolerable to be refused than deceived.

837. No good man ever grew rich all at once.

888. Forgetfulness is our only relief against losses.

839. Prosperity is ever providing itself with anxieties.

840. The greater our good fortune, the more likely to fail us.

841. Anger stops at nothing.

842. Accused innocence fears fate, not the witnesses.

843. It is not a hard lot to be obliged to return to the state whence we came.

844. I should not please to be king, if I must therefore be pleased to be cruel.

846. The hour of triumph loves no co-partnership.

846. You can obey a request much better than a command.

847. Everything is worth what its purchaser will pay for it.

848. Give your friend cause to blush; and you will be likely to lose him.

849. Repeated pardons encourage offenses.
850. To prefer a request smacks of servility to a noble spirit.
851. You would not sin so often if you knew some things of which you are ignorant.
852. The eyes and ears of the mob are often false witnesses.
853. Yon must buy a bushel of salt [with cash down] before you get credit.
854. It is right to injure a man to save his life.
855. There is no more sacred duty than to remember to whom you owe yourself.
856. When the wise man thinks, he arms himself against the assaults of the whole world.
857. The sage briefly refuses your request by his silence.
858. Folly is very often wisdom's companion.
859. Useful; and not multifarious knowledge, is wisdom.
860. Vain is that wisdom which does not profit the possessor.
861. You are eloquent enough if truth speaks through you.
862. Happy he who can die when he wishes.
863. It is enough to vanquish an enemy; more than enough to ruin him.
864. It is better to learn late than never.
865. Better be ignorant of a matter than half know it.
866. Better use medicines at the outset, than at the last moment.
867. The sons of the blacksmith are not frightened at sparks.
868. The judge is condemned when he punishes the innocent.
869. The angry think their power greater than it is.
870. Speak well of your friend in public, admonish him in secret.
871. Credit is poverty's good fortune.
872. Prosperity makes friends, adversity tries them.
873. The nurse's grief is almost as great as the mother's.
874. Sedition among the citizens is the enemy's opportunity.
875. He who has been once a criminal always passes for such.
876. Kindness of heart is always happy.
877. Human prudence ever fails when there is most need of it.
878. The wise man avoids evil by anticipating it.
879. Always shun whatever may make you angry.
880. Fear always comes back to curse its authors.
881. It is late to be devising expedients when the danger is at hand.

882. Bright faculties are the source of wisdom, not length of years.

883. It is late to guard against evil, when it has already come.

884. If you would fear nothing, fear everything.

885. If you are a mariner, let landsmen's business alone.

886. There will always be some to hate you, if you love yourself.

887. Vice is constrained to be its own curse.

888. To overthrow law, is to destroy our greatest protection.

889. He punishes himself who repents of his deeds.

890. He is the most hostile of enemies whose friendship is unreal.

891. The greatest of empires, is the empire over one's self.

892. The probity which is only assumed, is depravity doubly distilled.

893. Guilt's assistant is guilt's participant.

894. To have the universe bear one company, would be a great consolation in death.

895. In critical junctures, temerity is wont to take the place of prudence.

896. An hour sometimes restores us the sum of many years losses.

897. Glory is apt to follow when industry has prepared the road.

898. Our lives are apt to be meaner than our births.

899. There is hope of improvement so long as a man is alive to shame.

900. Hope is the solace of poverty, money of avarice, death of misery.

901. The sight of a thorn is pleasant when there is a rose by its side.

902. Fools stand in dread of fortune, wise men bear it.

903. It is folly to censure him whom all the world adores.

904. Prosperity sometimes exhibits a little folly.

905. Only fools commit the error which might have been avoided.

906. It is folly to take the uncertain for the certain.

907. It is foolish to complain of the misfortunes which have come to pass through your own fault.

908. It is folly to dread what cannot be avoided.

909. It is folly to take vengeance on another to your own injury.

910. It is folly to punish your neighbour by fire when you live next door.

911. Whom fortune wishes to destroy, she first makes mad.

912. It is folly for him to rule over others who cannot govern himself.

913. He is a fool who envies the happiness of the proud.

914. Let a fool hold his tongue, and he will pass for a sage.

915. He preserves his family's property who does not waste his own.
916. Benevolence tries persuasion first, and then severer measures.
917. A pleasant life this, if you know nothing; for ignorance is a pain-less evil.
918. The stolen ox sometimes puts his head out of the stall.
919. A lax government cannot maintain its authority
920. A boastful prosperity will prepare its own fall.
921. He favors the enemy who does not spare his own soldiers.
922. An ultra-right is generally an ultra-wrong.
923. The buyers of jewelry always suspect the quality of such ware.
924. Innocence always follows the guidance of its own light.
925. Suspicion of the worthy is a secret injustice done them.
926. We rarely incur danger by silence.
927. Avarice is as destitute of what it has, as what it has not.
928. Suspicion begets suspicion.
929. A suspicious mind distrusts the whole world.
930. He knows not when to be silent, who knows not when to speak.
931. Taciturnity is the dunce's wisdom.
932. As long as man is ignorant; so long he should be a learner.
933. He is much to be dreaded who stands in dread of poverty.
934. Timidity styles itself caution; stinginess frugality.
935. Sweet is the grievance when pleasure defers to profit.
936. Do not water your neighbor's fields when your own are parched.
937. It is disgraceful indigence which springs from extravagance.
938. It is a disgraceful loss which is chargeable to negligence.
939. When one man is protected [by law] all men are safe.
940. The highest safety is to fear naught but the Almighty.
941. The poor man is ruined as soon as he begins to ape the rich.
942. When you purchase another's property, you most part with some of your own.
943. Where destiny blunders, human prudence will not avail
944. When innocence trembles, it condemns the judge.
945. Where the accuser is the judge, power rules and not law.
946. When liberty has fallen, no one dares to open his mouth.
947. The greater your joys, the greater your occasion for fear.
948. When everybody is guilty, the prayer for relief will avail little.
949. When life is a continual terror, death is a blessing.
950. When the elder do wrong, the younger learn the lesson.

951. When caution keeps watch, naught comes to pass to be dreaded.

952. Where reverence dwells, there faith is ever kept.

953. The wounds of the soul should be cured before those of the body.

954. A single day executes the punishment, many prepared the way for it.

955. One will agree with you sooner than many.

956. It is right that one should perish that many may be saved.

957. We should use our friends while we have plenty of them.

958. The commander should foresee every contingency.

959. Even to be hung one should choose a fine tree.

960. Either be silent, or say something better than silence.

961. Penitence follows hasty decisions.

962. The importance of every word depends on the sense you give it.

963. Why do we not hear the truth? Because we don't speak it.

964. A lie is truth, when told for one's safety.

965. By tolerating an inveterate wrong, you invite a new one.

966. Vices often have a close relationship to virtues.

967. It is of advantage to be conquered when our own victory would be a loss.

968. You need not hang up the ivy branch over the wine that will sell.

969. The sound of a harp will not stay the flight of a fugitive.

970. A good man should not know how to do an injury.

971. You can accomplish by kindness what you cannot by force.

972. No one can honorably refuse to love virtue.

973. False modesty is an embarrassment to every virtue.

974. It is better to trust virtue than fortune.

975. Labor rejoices when it sees the rewards of virtue.

976. The semblance of courage gains a part of every victory.

977. It is nature, not his standing, that makes the good man.

978. Do not take a bad man for your companion on a journey.

979. Would you be known by everybody? Then you know nobody.

980. Life and reputation travel on with equal pace.

981. A life of leisure is a kingdom with less care [than a kingdom requires].

982. Fortune is mistress of life and not wisdom.

983. Conceal your opulence if you would avoid envy.

984. Vices grown inveterate are hard to correct.

985. Flattery was once a vice; now it is the fashion.

986. Every vice has its excuse ready.

987. Pride is prosperity's common vice.

988. Unchastity resides in the will, not in the body.

989. The sweetest pleasure arises from difficulties overcome.

990. There is more of fear than delight in a secret pleasure.

991. There is a great difference between seeming wise, and being so.

992. What has been given can be taken away.

993. The more skillful the gambler, the greater the scoundrel.

994. Sympathy in benevolence is the strongest of ties.

995. It is a consolation to the wretched to have companions in misery.

996. A good conscience never mutters mere Up-prayers.

997. A man of courage never endures an insult; an honorable man never offers one.

998. Even for wisdom it is a hard matter to bear affliction.

999. Any opportunity is a good one to him who thirsts for vengeance.

1000. The life of that man is detested by the citizens, whose death is expected by his friends.

1001. He is not considered a dupe who understood that he was deceived.

1002. Call a man an ingrate and you give him all manner of bad names in one.

1003. The service is twofold greater when it is promptly rendered.

1004. The little vices of the great must needs be accounted very great

1005. It is an advantage not to possess that which you must hold against your will.

1006. Disgrace is honorable when you die in a good cause.

1007. Cruel punishments do no honor to the king's majesty.

1008. The exile without a home is a dead man without sepulture.

1009. Anger would inflict punishment on another; meanwhile, it tortures itself.

1010. The happy man is not he who seems thus to others, but who seems thus to himself.

1011. Ton may despair of quiet; if you manage the affairs of women.

1012. Error and repentance are the attendants on hasty decisions.

1013. He who conquers his passions is a man of more nerve than he who subdues the enemy.

1014. In vain may you ask back your youth when old age has come on.

1015. The thunderbolt is forged when anger and power meet together.

1016. He finds assistance in adversity who renders services in prosperity.

1017. How terrible is that anguish which can find no voice amid tortures!

1018. How grievous to suffer at the hand of him of whom you dare not complain!

1019. It is a bitter dose to be taught obedience after you have learned to rule.

1020. How many causes for repentance do we find during a long life!

1021. Mercy to the afflicted is a [prudent] remembrance of one's self.

1022. We have one opinion of ourselves; and another of our neighbor.

1023. A single hour may often compensate for the losses of ten years.

1024. He who makes shipwreck a second time does wrong to accuse Neptune.

1025. None but the innocent in the midst of danger hope for good.

1026. It is harder to judge between friends than enemies.

1027. He who subdues his temper vanquishes his greatest enemy.

1028. Call yourself happy, and you invite the visits of misfortune.

1029. Fear the envy of your friends more than the snares of your enemies.

1030. Malice swallows the greater part of its own venom.

1031. There is the greatest danger in guarding what the multitude covet.

1032. I am not your friend unless I share in your fortunes.

1033. Death is a blessing to infancy, bitter for youth, too tardy for old age.

1034. We simply rob ourselves when we make presents to the dead.

1035. A single instant brings much to pass that no one dreams of.

1036. Great hatred can be concealed in the countenance, and much in a kiss.

1037. Verily he abounds in virtues who [merely] loves those of others.

1038. Count not him among your friends who will retail your privacies to the world.

1039. Do not be too hasty in accusing, or approving any one.

1040. You know neither what to hope or fear; you are the sport of a day.

1041. He can do no harm who has lost the desire to do it.

1042. Unless degree is preserved, the first place is safe for no one.

1043. It is no profit to have learned well, if you neglect to do well.

1044. Reason avails nothing when passion has the mastery.

1045. There is no problem so difficult that it cannot be solved by investigation.

1046. You should not lead one life in private and another in public.

1047. You are not yet happy if the rabble do not make sport of you.

1048. The house is by no means straightened that holds many friends.

1049. There is no fortune so good that you cannot complain of it.

1050. No where can we die happier then where we have lived happily.

1051. Reproaches in misfortune are more intolerable than misfortune itself.

1052. Hatred of evil should constrain you to right, not fear.

1053. Death ever uncertain gets the start of such as are always beginning to live.

1054. A service is well rendered when the receiver can remember it

1055. It is very well to imitate our ancestors, if they led in the right way.

1056. The crime of the parent should never be a prejudice to the son.

1057. Money is a servant if you know how to use it; if not, it is a master.

1058. When we speak evil of others, we generally condemn ourselves.

1059. To apply a common fund to our individual uses is the beginning of discord.

1060. Confession of our faults is the next thing to innocence.

1061. The later in life evil courses are begun, the more disgraceful they are.

1062. When you cannot restrain a man by kindness, try something else.

1063. It is an embarrassment to the possessor to have more than he needs.

1064. What matters it how much you have? There is more which you cannot have.

1065. The same man can rarely say a great deal and say it to the purpose.

1066. Much harder is the lot of kings than that of their subjects.

1067. Not the criminals; but their crimes it is well to extirpate.

1068. In our hatred of guilty it is folly to ruin innocence.

1069. It is often better to overlook an injury than avenge it.

1070. I have-often regretted my speech, never my silence.

1071. You had better please one good man than many bad ones.

1072. Keep the golden mean, between saying too much and too little.

1073. Speech is a mirror of the soul; as a man speaks, so is he.

1074. If you obey against your will, you are a slave; if of your will, you are an assistant.

1075. Let your life be pleasing to the multitude, and it cannot be so to yourself.

1076. If you gain new friends, don't forget the old ones.

1077. There is no pain in the wound received in the moment of victory.

1078. If you would live innocently, seek solitude.

1079. Avarice is as destitute of what it has, as poverty of what it has not.

1080. There is as much cruelty in pardoning all, as in pardoning none.

1081. He lays up his treasure in a sepulcher who makes an old man his heir.

1082. It is a less evil to be unable to live than not to know how to live.

1083. A sentence to death is more tolerable than a command to live wickedly.

1084. An evil conscience is often quiet, but never secure.

1085. Away from your country, though in the midst of friends, you long to return thither again.

1086. When the dog is too old you cannot get him used to the collar.

1087. Man's life is short; and therefore an honorable death is his immortality.

Life of Antisthenes

By

Diogenes Laërtius

I. ANTISTHENES was an Athenian, the son of Antisthenes. And he was said not to be a legitimate Athenian; in reference to which he said to someone who was reproaching him with the circumstance, "The mother of the Gods too is a Phrygian;" for he was thought to have had a Thracian mother.

On which account, as he had borne himself bravely in the battle of Tanagra, he gave occasion to Socrates to say that the son of two Athenians could not have been so brave. And he himself, when disparaging the Athenians who gave themselves great airs as having been born out of the earth itself, said that they were not more noble as far as that went than snails and locusts.

II. Originally he was a pupil of Gorgias the rhetorician; owing to which circumstance he employs the rhetorical style of language in his *Dialogues*, especially in his *Truth* and in his *Exhortations*. And Hermippus says, that he had originally intended in his address at the assembly, on account of the Isthmian games, to attack and also to praise the Athenians, and Thebans, and Lacedaemonians; but that he afterwards abandoned the design, when he saw that there were a great many spectators come from those cities. Afterwards, he attached himself to Socrates, and made such progress in philosophy while with him, that he advised all his own pupils to become his fellow pupils in the school of Socrates. And as he lived in the Piraeus, he went up forty furlongs to the city every day, in order to hear Socrates, from whom he learnt the art of enduring, and of being indifferent to external circumstances, and so became the original founder of the Cynic school.

III. And he used to argue that labour was a good thing, by adducing the examples of the great Hercules, and of Cyrus, one of which he derived from the Greeks and the other from the barbarians.

IV. He was also the first person who ever gave a definition of discourse, saying, "Discourse is that which shows what anything is or was." And he used continually to say, "I would rather go mad than feel pleasure." And, "One ought to attach one's self to such women as will thank one for it." He said once to a youth from Pontus, who was on the point of coming to him to be his pupil, and was asking him what things he wanted, "You want a new book, and a new pen, and a new tablet;" meaning a new mind. And to a person who asked him from what country he had better marry a wife, he said, "If you marry a handsome woman, she will be common; if an ugly woman, she will be a punishment to you."

He was told once that Plato spoke ill of him, and he replied, "It is a royal privilege to do well, and to be evil spoken of."

When he was being initiated into the mysteries of Orpheus, and the priest said that those who were initiated enjoyed many good things in the shades below, "Why, then," said he "do not you die?" Being once reproached as not being the son of two free citizens, he said, "And I am not the son of two people skilled in wrestling; nevertheless, I am a skillful wrestler." On one occasion he was asked why he had but few disciples, and said, "Because I drove them away with a silver rod." When he was asked why he reproved his pupils with bitter language, he said, "Physicians too use severe remedies for their patients." Once he saw an adulterer running away, and said, "unhappy man! how much danger could you have avoided for one obol!" He used to say, as Hecaton tells us in his *Apophthegms*, "That it was better to fall among crows, than among flatterers; for that they only devour the dead, but the others devour the living." When he was asked what was the most happy event that could take place in human life, he said, "To die while prosperous."

On one occasion one of his friends was lamenting to him that he had lost his memoranda, and he said to him, "You ought to have written them on your mind, and not on paper."

A favourite saying of his was, "That envious people were devoured by their own disposition, just as iron is by rust." Another was, "That those who wish to be immortal ought to live piously and justly."

He used to say too, "That cities were ruined when they were unable to distinguish worthless citizens from virtuous ones." On one occasion he was being praised by some wicked men, and said, "I am sadly afraid that I must have done some wicked thing." One of his favourite sayings was, "That the fellowship of brothers of one mind was stronger than any fortified city." He used to say, "That those things were the best for a man to take on a journey, which would float with him if he were shipwrecked." He was once reproached for being intimate with wicked men, and said, "Physicians also live with those who are sick; and yet they do not catch fevers."

He used to say, "that it was an absurd thing to clean a cornfield of tares, and in war to get rid of bad soldiers, and yet not to rid one's self in a city of the wicked citizens." When he was asked what advantage he had ever derived from philosophy, he replied, "The advantage of being able to converse with myself." At a drinking party, a man once said to him, "Give us a song," and he replied, "Do you play us a tune on the flute." When Diogenes asked him for a tunic, he bade him fold his cloak. He was asked on one occasion what learning was the most necessary, and he replied, "To unlearn one's bad habits." And he used to exhort those who found themselves ill spoken of, to endure it more than they would any one's throwing stones at them. He used to laugh at Plato as conceited; accordingly, once when there was a fine procession, seeing a horse neighing, he said to Plato, "I think you too would be a very frisky horse," and he said this all the more, because Plato kept continually praising the horse. At another time, he had gone to see him when he was ill, and when he saw there a dish in which Plato had been sick, he said, "I see your bile there, but I do not see your conceit."

He used to advise the Athenians to pass a vote that asses were horses; and, as they thought that irrational, he said, "Why, those whom you make generals have never learnt to be really generals, they have only been voted such."

A man said to him one day, "Many people praise you."

"Why, what evil," said he, "have I done?"

When he turned the rent in his cloak outside, Socrates seeing it, said to him, "I see your vanity through the hole in your cloak."

On another occasion, the question was put to him by some one, as Phanias relates, in his treatise *On the Philosophers of the Socratic*

School, what a man could do to show himself an honourable and a virtuous man; and he replied, "If you attend to those who understand the subject, and learn from them that you ought to shun the bad habits which you have."

Some one was praising luxury in his hearing, and he said, "May the children of my enemies be luxurious." Seeing a young man place himself in a carefully studied attitude before a modeller, he said, "Tell me, if the brass could speak, on what would it pride itself?" And when the young man replied, "On its beauty." "Are you not then," said he, "ashamed to rejoice in the same thing as an inanimate piece of brass?"

A young man from Pontus once promised to recollect him, if a vessel of salt fish arrived; and so he took him with him, and also an empty bag, and went to a woman who sold meal, and filled his sack and went away; and when the woman asked him to pay for it, he said, "The young man will pay you, when the vessel of salt fish comes home."

He it was who appears to have been the cause of Anytus's banishment, and of Meletus's death. For having met with some young men of Pontus, who had come to Athens, on account of the reputation of Socrates, he took them to Anytus, telling them, that in moral philosophy he was wiser than Socrates; and they who stood by were indignant at this, and drove him away. And whenever he saw a woman beautifully adorned, he would go off to her house, and desire her husband to bring forth his horse and his arms; and then if he had such things, he would give him leave to indulge in luxury, for that he had the means of defending himself; but if he had them not, then he would bid him strip his wife of her ornaments.

V. And the doctrines he adopted were these. He used to insist that virtue was a thing which might be taught; also, that the nobly born and virtuously disposed, were the same people; for that virtue was of itself sufficient for happiness, and was in need of nothing, except the strength of Socrates. He also looked upon virtue as a species of work, not wanting many arguments, or much instruction; and he taught that the wise man was sufficient for himself; for that everything that belonged to anyone else belonged to him. He considered obscurity of fame a good thing, and equally good with labour. And he used to say that the wise man would regulate his conduct as a citizen, not according to the established laws of the state, but according to the law of virtue. And that he would marry for the sake of having children, selecting the most beautiful woman for his wife. And that he would love her; for that the wise man alone knew what objects deserved love.

Diocles also attributes the following apothegms to him:

To the wise man, nothing is strange and nothing remote.

The virtuous man is worthy to be loved.

Good men are friends. It is right to make the brave and just one's allies.

Virtue is a weapon of which a man cannot be deprived.

It is better to fight with a few good men against all the wicked, than with many wicked men against a few good men.

One should attend to one's enemies, for they are the first persons to detect one's errors.

One should consider a just man as of more value than a relation.

Virtue is the same in a man as in a woman.

What is good is honourable, and what is bad is disgraceful.

Think everything that is wicked, foreign.

Prudence is the safest fortification; for it can neither fall to pieces nor be betrayed.

One must prepare one's self a fortress in one's own impregnable thoughts.

VI. He used to lecture in the Gymnasium, called Cynosarges, not far from the gates; and some people say that it is from that place that the sect got the name of Cynics. And he himself was called Haplocyon ('downright dog').

VII. He was the first person to set the fashion of doubling his cloak, as Diocles says, and he wore no other garment. And he used to carry a stick and a wallet; but Neanthes says that he was the first person who wore a cloak without folding it. But Sosicrates, in the third book of his *Successions*, says that Diodorus, of Aspendos, let his beard grow, and used to carry a stick and a wallet.

VIII. He is the only one of all the pupils of Socrates, whom Theopompus praises and speaks of as clever, and able to persuade whomsoever he pleased by the sweetness of his conversation. And this is plain, both from his own writings, and from *The Banquet* of Xenophon. He appears to have been the founder of the more manly

Stoic school; on which account Athenasus, the epigrammatist, speaks thus of them:

Ye, who learned are in Stoic fables,
Ye who consign the wisest of all doctrines
To your most sacred books; you say that virtue
Is the sole good; for that alone can save
The life of man, and strongly fenced cities.
But if some fancy pleasure their best aim,
One of the Muses 'tis who has convinc'd them.

He was the original cause of the apathy of Diogenes, and the temperance of Crates, and the patience of Zeno, having himself, as it were, laid the foundations of the city which they afterwards built. And Xenophon says, that in his conversation and society, he was the most delightful of men, and in every respect the most temperate.

IX. There are ten volumes of his writings extant. The first volume is that in which there is the essay *On Style*, or *On Figures of Speech*; *The Ajax*, or *Speech of Ajax*; *The Defence of Orestes* or the treatise *On Lawyers*; *The Isographe*, or *The Lysiasarid Isocrates*; the reply to the work of Isocrates, entitled *The Absence of Witnesses*. The second volume is that in which we have the treatise *On the Nature of Animals*; *On the Procreation of Children, or On Marriage*, an essay of an amatory character; *On the Sophists*, an essay of a physiognomic character; *On Justice and Manly Virtue*, being three essays of an hortatory character; two treatises on Theognis. The third volume contains a treatise *On the Good; On Manly Courage; On Law, or Political Constitutions; On Law, or What is Honourable and Just; On Freedom and Slavery; On Good Faith; On a Guardian, or On Persuasion; On Victory*, an economical essay. The fourth volume contains *The Cyrus; The Greater Heracles, or a treatise on Strength*. The fifth volume contains *The Cyrus, or a treatise on Kingly Power; The Aspasia*.

The sixth volume is that in which there is the treatise *Truth*; another (a disputatious one) *Concerning Arguing*; the *Sathon, or on Contradiction*, in three parts; and an essay *On Dialect*. The seventh contains a treatise on *Education, or Names*, in five books; one on the *Use of Names, or the Contentious Man*; one *On Questions and Answers*; one *On Opinion and Knowledge*, in four books; one *On Dying*;

one *On Life and Death*; one on those who are in the Shades below; one on Nature, in two books; two books of *Questions in Natural Philosophy*; one essay, called *Opinions on the Contentious Man*; one book *Of Problems*, on the subject of *Learning*. The eighth volume is that in which we find a treatise on *Music*; one on *Interpreters*; one on *Homer*; one on *Injustice and Impiety*; one on Calchas; one on a Spy; one on Pleasure. The ninth book contains an essay on *The Odyssey*; one on *The Magic Wand; The Minerva*, or an essay on Telemachus; an essay on Helen and Penelope; one on Proteus; the Cyclops, being an essay on Ulysses; an essay on *The Use of Wine, or on Drunkenness, or on the Cyclops*; one on Circe; one on Amphiaraus; one on Ulysses and Penelope, and also on Ulysses' Dog. The tenth volume is occupied by the Heracles, or Medas; the Hercules, or an *Essay on Prudence or Strength*; *The Lord or the Lover; The Lord or the Spies*; *The Menexenus, or an essay on Governing*; *The Alcibiades*; *The Archelaus, or an essay on Kingly Power*. These then are the names of his works. And Timon, rebuking him because of their great number, called him a universal chatterer.

X. He died of some disease; and while he was ill Diogenes came to visit him, and said to him, "Have you no need of a friend?" Once too he came to see him with a sword in his hand; and when Antisthenes said, "Who can deliver me from this suffering?" he, pointing to the sword, said, "This can;" But he rejoined, "I said from suffering, but not from life;" for he seemed to bear his disease the more calmly from his love of life. And there is an epigram on him written by ourselves, which runs thus:

> *In life you were a bitter dog, Antisthenes,*
> *Born to bite people's minds with sayings sharp,*
> *Not with your actual teeth. Now you are slain*
> *By fell consumption, passersby may say,*
> *Why should he not, one wants a guide to Hell.*

There were also three other people of the name of Antisthenes. One, a disciple of Heraclitus; the second, an Ephesian; the third, a historian of Rhodes.

The Symposium: Book IV

By

Xenophon

Translated by H. G. Dakyns

At this point, Socrates took up the conversation:

It now devolves on us to prove in turn that what we each have undertaken to defend is really valuable.

Then Callias:

Be pleased to listen to me first: My case is this, that while the rest of you go on debating what justice and uprightness are, I spend my time in making men more just and upright.

Soc. And how do you do that, good sir?

Call. By giving money, to be sure.

Antisthenes sprang to his feet at once, and with the manner of a cross-examiner demanded: Do human beings seem to you to harbour justice in their souls, or in their purses, Callias?

Call. In their souls.

Ant. And do you pretend to make their souls more righteous by putting money in their pockets?

Call. Undoubtedly.

Ant. Pray how?

Call. In this way. When they know that they are furnished with the means, that is to say, my money, to buy necessaries, they would rather not incur the risk of evil-doing, and why should they?

Ant. And pray, do they repay you these same moneys?

Call. I cannot say they do.

Ant. Well then, do they requite your gifts of gold with gratitude?

Call. No, not so much as a bare "Thank you." In fact, some of them are even worse disposed towards me when they have got my money than before.

Now, here's a marvel! (exclaimed Antisthenes, and as he spoke he eyed the witness with an air of triumph). You can render people just to all the world, but towards yourself you cannot?

Pray, where's the wonder? (asked the other). Do you not see what scores of carpenters and house-builders there are who spend their time in building houses for half the world; but for themselves they simply cannot do it, and are forced to live in lodgings. And so admit that home-thrust, Master Sophist; and confess yourself confuted.

Upon my soul, he had best accept his fate (said Socrates). Why, after all, you are only like those prophets who proverbially foretell the future for mankind, but cannot foresee what is coming upon themselves.

And so the first discussion ended.

Thereupon Niceratus: Lend me your ears, and I will tell you in what respects you shall be better for consorting with myself. I presume, without my telling you, you know that Homer, being the wisest of mankind, has touched upon nearly every human topic in his poems. Whosoever among you, therefore, would fain be skilled in economy, or oratory, or strategy; whose ambition it is to be like Achilles, or Ajax, Nestor, or Odysseus—one and all pay court to me, for I have all this knowledge at my fingers' ends.

Pray (interposed Antisthenes), do you also know the way to be a king? since Homer praises Agamemnon, you are well aware, as being a goodly king and eke a spearman bold or, "Have you the knowledge also how to play the king?"

Nic. Full well I know it, and full well I know the duty of a skilful charioteer; how he who holds the ribbons must turn his chariot nigh the pillar's edge, himself inclined upon the polished chariot-board. A little to the left of the twin pair: the right hand horse touch with the prick, and shout a cheery shout, and give him rein. I know another thing besides, and you may put it to the test this instant, if you like. Homer somewhere has said: *And at his side an onion, which to drink gives relish.* So if someone will but bring an onion, you shall reap the benefit of my sage lore in less than no time, and your wine will taste the sweeter.

Here Charmides exclaimed: Good sirs, let me explain. Niceratus is anxious to go home, redolent of onions, so that his fair lady may persuade herself, it never entered into anybody's head to kiss her lord.

Bless me, that isn't all (continued Socrates); if we do not take care, we shall win ourselves a comic reputation. A relish must it be, in very truth, that can sweeten cup as well as platter, this same onion; and if we are to take to munching onions for desert, see if somebody does not say of us, "They went to dine with Callias, and got more than their deserts, the epicures."

No fear of that (rejoined Niceratus). Always take a bite of onion before speeding forth to battle, just as your patrons of the cock-pit give their birds a feed of garlic before they put them for the fight. But for ourselves our thoughts are less intent perhaps on dealing blows than blowing kisses.

Chorus. And here's the garlic. Swallow it down! Sausage Seller.... What for? Chorus. It will prime you up and make you fight the better.

After such sort the theme of their discourse reached its conclusion.

Then Critobulus spoke: It is now my turn, I think, to state to you the grounds on which I pride myself on beauty.

A chorus of voices rejoined: Say on.

Crit. To begin with, if I am not beautiful, as methinks I be, you will bring on your own heads the penalty of perjury; for, without waiting to have the oath administered, you are always taking the gods to witness that you find me beautiful. And I must needs believe you, for are you not all honourable men? If I then be so beautiful and affect you, even as I also am affected by him whose fair face here attracts me, I swear by all the company of heaven I would not choose the great king's empire in exchange for what I am—the beauty of the world, the paragon of animals. And at this instant I feast my eyes on Cleinias gladlier than on all other sights which men deem fair. Joyfully will I welcome blindness to all else, if but these eyes may still behold him and him only. With sleep and night I am sore vexed, which rob me of his sight; but to daylight and the sun I owe eternal thanks, for they restore him to me, my heart's joy.

Cleinias. Yes, and herein also have we, the beautiful, just claim to boast. The strong man may by dint of toil obtain good things; the brave, by danger boldly faced, and the wise by eloquence of speech; but to the beautiful alone it is given to achieve all ends in absolute quiescence. To take myself as an example. I know that riches are a sweet possession, yet sweeter far to me to give all that I have to Cleinias than to receive a fortune from another. Gladly would I become a slave—ay, forfeit freedom—if Cleinias would deign to be my lord. Toil in his service were easier for me than rest from labour: danger incurred in his behalf far sweeter than security of days. So that if you, Callias, may boast of making men more just and upright, to me belongs by juster right than yours to train mankind to every excellence. We are the true inspirers who infuse some subtle fire into amorous souls, we beauties, and thereby raise them to new heights of being; we render them more liberal in the pursuit of wealth; we give them a zest for toil that mocks at danger, and enables them where honour the fair vision leads, to follow. We fill their souls with deeper modesty, a self-constraint more staunch; about the things they care for most, there floats a halo of protecting awe. Fools and unwise are they who choose not beauteous men to be their generals. How merrily would I, at any rate, march through fire by the side of Cleinias; and so would all of you, I know full well, in company of him who now addresses you.

Cease, therefore, your perplexity, O Socrates, abandon fears and doubts, believe and know that this thing of which I make great boast, my beauty, has power to confer some benefit on humankind.

Once more, let no man dare dishonour beauty, merely because the flower of it soon fades, since even as a child has growth in beauty, so is it with the stripling, the grown man, the reverend senior. And this the proof of my contention. Whom do we choose to bear the sacred olive-shoot in honour of Athena?—whom else save beautiful old men? witnessing thereby that beauty walks hand in hand as a companion with every age of life, from infancy to eld.

Or again, if it be sweet to win from willing hearts the things we seek for, I am persuaded that, by the eloquence of silence, I could win a kiss from yonder girl or boy more speedily than ever you could, O sage! by help of half a hundred subtle arguments.

Eh, bless my ears, what's that? (Socrates broke in upon this final flourish of the speaker). So beautiful you claim to rival me, you boaster?

Crit. Why, yes indeed, I hope so, or else I should be uglier than all the Silenuses in the Satyric drama. Good! (Socrates rejoined); the moment the programme of discussion is concluded, please remember, we must obtain a verdict on the point of beauty. Judgment shall be given—not at the bar of Alexander, son of Priam—but of these who, as you flatter yourself, have such a hankering to kiss you.

Oh, Socrates (he answered, deprecatingly), will you not leave it to the arbitrament of Cleinias?

Then Socrates: Will you never tire of repeating that one name? It is Cleinias here, there, and everywhere with you.

Crit. And if his name died on my lips, think you my mind would less recall his memory? Know you not, I bear so clear an image of him in my soul, that had I the sculptor's or the limner's skill, I might portray his features as exactly from this image of the mind as from contemplation of his actual self.

But Socrates broke in: Pray, why then, if you bear about this lively image, why do you give me so much trouble, dragging me to this and that place, where you hope to see him?

Crit. For this good reason, Socrates, the sight of him inspires gladness, whilst his phantom brings not joy so much as it engenders longing.

At this point Hermogenes protested: I find it most unlike you, Socrates, to treat thus negligently one so passion-crazed as Critobulus.

Socrates replied: Do you suppose the sad condition of the patient dates from the moment only of our intimacy?

Herm. Since when, then?

Soc. Since when? Why, look at him: the down begins to mantle on his cheeks, and on the nape of Cleinias' neck already mounts. The fact is, when they fared to the same school together, he caught the fever. This his father was aware of, and consigned him to me, hoping I might be able to do something for him. Ay, and his plight is not so sorry now. Once he would stand agape at him like one whose gaze is fixed upon the Gorgons, his eyes one stony stare, and like a stone himself turn heavily away. But nowadays I have seen the statue actually blink. And yet, may Heaven help me! my good sirs, I think, between ourselves, the culprit must have bestowed a kiss on Cleinias, than which love's flame asks no fiercer fuel. So insatiable a thing it is and so suggestive of mad fantasy. (And for this reason held perhaps in higher honour, because of all external acts the close of lip with lip bears the same name as that of soul with soul in love.) Wherefore, say I, let every one who wishes to be master of himself and sound of soul abstain from kisses imprinted on fair lips.

Then Charmides: Oh! Socrates, why will you scare your friends with these hobgoblin terrors, bidding us all beware of handsome faces, whilst you yourself—yes, by Apollo, I will swear I saw you at the schoolmaster's that time when both of you were poring over one book, in which you searched for something, you and Critobulus, head to head, shoulder to shoulder bare, as if incorporate? As yes, alack the day! (he answered); and that is why, no doubt, my shoulder ached for more than five days afterwards, as if I had been bitten by some fell beast, and me thought I felt a sort of scraping at the heart. Now therefore, in the presence of these witnesses, I warn you, Critobulus, never again to touch me till you wear as thick a crop of hair upon your chin as on your head.

So pell-mell they went at it, half jest half earnest, and so the medley ended. Callias here called on Charmides.

Call. Now, Charmides, it lies with you to tell us why you pride yourself on poverty.

Charmides responded: On all hands it is admitted, I believe, that confidence is better than alarm; better to be a freeman than a slave; better to be worshipped than pay court to others; better to be trusted than to be suspected by one's country.

Well now, I will tell you how it fared with me in this same city when I was wealthy. First, I lived in daily terror lest some burglar should break into my house and steal my goods and do myself some injury. I cringed before informers. I was obliged to pay these people court, because I knew that I could injure them far less than they could injure me. Never-ending the claims upon my pocket which the state enforced upon me; and as to setting foot abroad, that was beyond the range of possibility. But now that I have lost my property across the frontier, and derive no income from my lands in Attica itself; now that my very household goods have been sold up, I stretch my legs at ease, I get a good night's rest. The distrust of my fellow-citizens has vanished; instead of trembling at threats, it is now my turn to threaten; at last I feel myself a freeman, with liberty to go abroad or stay at home as suits my fancy. The tables now are turned. It is the rich who rise to give me their seats, who stand aside and make way for me as I meet them in the streets. To-day I am like a despot, yesterday I was literally a slave; formerly it was I who had to pay my tribute to the sovereign people, now it is I who am supported by the state by means of general taxation.

And there is another thing. So long as I was rich, they threw in my teeth as a reproach that I was friends with Socrates, but now that I am become a beggar no one troubles his head two straws about the matter. Once more, the while I rolled in plenty I had everything to lose, and, as a rule, I lost it; what the state did not exact, some mischance stole from me. But now that is over. I lose nothing, having nought to lose; but, on the contrary, I have everything to gain, and live in hope of some day getting something. Call. And so, of course, your one prayer is that you may never more be rich, and if you are visited by a dream of luck your one thought is to offer sacrifice to Heaven to avert misfortune.

Char. No, that I do not. On the contrary, I run my head into each danger most adventurously. I endure, if haply I may see a chance of getting something from some quarter of the sky some day.

Come now (Socrates exclaimed), it lies with you, sir, you, Antisthenes, to explain to us, how it is that you, with means so scanty, make so loud a boast of wealth.

Because (he answered) I hold to the belief, sirs, that wealth and poverty do not lie in a man's estate, but in men's souls. Even in private life how many scores of people have I seen, who, although they roll in wealth, yet deem themselves so poor, there is nothing they will shrink from, neither toil nor danger, in order to add a little to their store. I have known two brothers, heirs to equal fortunes, one of whom has enough, more than enough, to cover his expenditure; the other is in absolute indigence. And so to monarchs, there are not a few, I perceive, so ravenous of wealth that they will outdo the veriest vagrants in atrocity. Want prompts a thousand crimes, you must admit. Why do men steal? why break burglariously into houses? why hale men and women captive and make slaves of them? Is it not from want? Nay, there are monarchs who at one fell swoop destroy whole houses, make wholesale massacre, and oftentimes reduce entire states to slavery, and all for the sake of wealth. These I must needs pity for the cruel malady which plagues them. Their condition, to my mind, resembles that poor creature's who, in spite of all he has and all he eats, can never stay the wolf that gnaws his vitals.

But as to me, my riches are so plentiful I cannot lay my hands on them myself; yet for all that I have enough to eat till my hunger is stayed, to drink till my thirst is sated; to clothe myself withal; and out of doors not Callias there, with all his riches, is more safe than I from shivering; and when I find myself indoors, what warmer shirting do I need than my bare walls? what ampler greatcoat than the tiles above my head? these seem to suit me well enough; and as to bedclothes, I am not so ill supplied but it is a business to arouse me in the morning.

Well then, these several pleasures I enjoy so fully that I am much more apt to pray for less than more of them, so strongly do I feel that some of them are sweeter than what is good for one or profitable.

But of all the precious things in my possession, I reckon this the choicest, that were I robbed of my whole present stock, there is no work so mean, but it would amply serve me to furnish me with sustenance. Why, look you, whenever I desire to fare delicately, I have not to purchase precious viands in the market, which becomes expensive, but I open the storehouse of my soul, and dole them out. Indeed, as far as pleasure goes, I find it better to await desire before I suffer meat or drink to pass my lips, than to have recourse to any of your costly viands, as, for instance, now, when I have chanced on this fine Thasian wine, and sip it without thirst. But indeed, the man who makes frugality, not wealth of worldly goods, his aim, is on the face of it a much more upright person. And why?—the man who is content with what he has will least of all be prone to clutch at what is his neighbour's.

And here's a point worth noting. Wealth of my sort will make you liberal of soul. Look at Socrates; from him it was I got these riches. He did not supply me with it by weight or by measure, but just as much as I could carry, he with bounteous hand consigned to me. And I, too, grudge it to no man now. To all my friends without distinction I am ready to display my opulence: come one, come all; and whosoever likes to take a share is welcome to the wealth that lies within my soul. Yes, and moreover, that most luxurious of possessions, unbroken leisure, you can see, is mine, which leaves me free to contemplate things worthy of contemplation, and to drink in with my ears all charming sounds. And what I value most, freedom to spend whole days in pure scholastic intercourse with Socrates, to whom I am devoted. And he, on his side, is not the person to admire those whose tale of gold and silver happens to be the largest, but those who are well-pleasing to him he chooses for companions, and will consort with to the end.

With these words the speaker ended, and Callias exclaimed:

By Hera, I envy you your wealth, Antisthenes, firstly, because the state does not lay burthens on you and treat you like a slave; and secondly, people do not fall into a rage with you when you refuse to be their creditor.

You may stay your envy (interposed Niceratus), I shall presently present myself to borrow of him this same key of his to independence. Trained as I am to cast up figures by my master Homer—

Seven tripods, which ne'er felt the fire, and of gold ten talents
And burnished braziers twenty, and horses twelve—

by weight and measure duly reckoned, I cannot stay my craving for enormous wealth. And that's the reason certain people, I daresay, imagine I am inordinately fond of riches.

The remark drew forth a peal of laughter from the company, who thought the speaker hit the truth exactly.

Then some one: It lies with you, Hermogenes, to tell us who your friends are; and next, to demonstrate the greatness of their power and their care for you, if you would prove to us your right to pride yourself on them.

Herm. That the gods know all things, that the present and the future lie before their eyes, are tenets held by Hellenes and barbarians alike. This is obvious; or else, why do states and nations, one and all, inquire of the gods by divination what they ought to do and what they ought not? This also is apparent, that we believe them able to do us good and to do us harm; or why do all men pray to Heaven to avert the evil and bestow the good? Well then, my boast is that these gods, who know and can do all things, deign to be my friends; so that, by reason of their care for me, I can never escape from their sight, neither by night nor by day, whithersoever I essay to go, whatsoever I take in hand to do. But because they know beforehand the end and issue of each event, they give me signals, sending messengers, be it some voice, or vision of the night, with omens of the solitary bird, which tell me what I should and what I should not do. When I listen to their warnings all goes well with me, I have no reason to repent; but if, as ere now has been the case, I have been disobedient, chastisement has overtaken me.

Then Socrates: All this I well believe, but there is one thing I would gladly learn of you: What service do you pay the gods, so to secure their friendship?

Truly it is not a ruinous service, Socrates (he answered)—far from it. I give them thanks, which is not costly. I make return to them of all they give to me from time to time. I speak well of them, with all the strength I have. And whenever I take their sacred names to witness, I do not wittingly falsify my word.

Then God be praised (said Socrates), if being what you are, you have such friends; the gods themselves, it would appear, delight in nobleness of soul.

Thus, in solemn sort, the theme was handled, thus gravely ended.

But now it was the jester's turn, and so they fell to asking him: What could he see to pride himself upon so vastly in the art of making people laugh?

Surely I have good reason (he replied). The whole world knows my business is to set them laughing, so when they are in luck's way, they eagerly invite me to a share of it; but if ill betide them, helter-skelter off they go, and never once turn back, so fearful are they I may set them laughing willy-nilly.

Nic. Heavens! you have good reason to be proud; with me it is just the opposite. When any of my friends are doing well, they take good care to turn their backs on me, but if ever it goes ill with them, they claim relationship by birth, and will not let their long-lost cousin out of sight.

Charm. Well, well! and you, sir (turning to the Syracusan), what do you pride yourself upon? No doubt, upon the boy?

The Syr. Not I, indeed; I am terribly afraid concerning him. It is plain enough to me that certain people are contriving for his ruin.

Good gracious! (Socrates exclaimed, when he heard that), what crime can they conceive your boy is guilty of that they should wish to make an end of him?

The Syr. I do not say they want to murder him, but wheedle him away with bribes to pass his nights with them.

Soc. And if that happened, you on your side, it appears, believe the boy will be corrupted?

The Syr. Beyond all shadow of a doubt, most villainously.

Soc. And you, of course, you never dream of such a thing. You don't spend nights with him?

The Syr. Of course I do, all night and every night.

Soc. By Hera, what a mighty piece of luck for you—to be so happily compounded, of such flesh and blood. You alone can't injure those who sleep beside you. You have every right, it seems, to boast of your own flesh, if nothing else.

The Syr. Nay, in sooth, it is not on that I pride myself.

Soc. Well, on what then?

The Syr. Why, on the silly fools who come and see my puppet show. I live on them.

Phil. Ah yes! and that explains how the other day I heard you praying to the gods to grant you, wheresoe'er you chance to be, great store of corn and wine, but dearth of wits.

Pass on (said Callias); now it is your turn, Socrates. What have you to say to justify your choice? How can you boast of so discredited an art?

He answered: Let us first decide what are the duties of the good go-between; and please to answer every question without hesitating; let us know the points to which we mutually assent. Are you agreed to that?

The Company, in chorus. Without a doubt (they answered, and the formula, once started, was every time repeated by the company, full chorus).

Soc. Are you agreed it is the business of a good go-between to make him (or her) on whom he plies his art agreeable to those with them?

Omnes. Without a doubt.

Soc. And, further, that towards agreeableness, one step at any rate consists in wearing a becoming fashion of the hair and dress? Are you agreed to that?

Omnes. Without a doubt.

Soc. And we know for certain, that with the same eyes a man may dart a look of love or else of hate on those he sees. Are you agreed?

Omnes. Without a doubt.

Soc. Well! and with the same tongue and lips and voice may speak with modesty or boastfulness?

Omnes. Without a doubt.

Soc. And there are words that bear the stamp of hate, and words that tend to friendliness?

Omnes. Without a doubt.

Soc. The good go-between will therefore make his choice between them, and teach only what conduces to agreeableness?

Omnes. Without a doubt.

Soc. And is he the better go-between who can make his clients pleasing to one person only, or can make them pleasing to a number?

The company was here divided; the one half answered, "Yes, of course, the largest number," whilst the others still maintained, "Without a doubt."

And Socrates, remarking, "That proposition is agreed to also," thus proceeded: And if further he were able to make them pleasing to the whole community, should we not have found in this accomplished person an arch-go-between?

Clearly so (they answered with one voice).

Soc. If then a man had power to make his clients altogether pleasing; that man, I say, might justly pride himself upon his art, and should by rights receive a large reward?

And when these propositions were agreed to also, he turned about and said: Just such a man, I take it, is before you in the person of Antisthenes!

Whereupon Antisthenes exclaimed: What! are you going to pass on the business? will you devolve this art of yours on me as your successor, Socrates?

I will, upon my word, I will (he answered): since I see that you have practised to some purpose, nay elaborated, an art which is the handmaid to this other.

And what may that be? asked Antisthenes.

Soc. The art of the procurer.

The other (in a tone of deep vexation): Pray, what thing of the sort are you aware I ever perpetrated?

Soc. I am aware that it was you who introduced our host here, Callias, to that wise man Prodicus; they were a match, you saw, the one enamoured of philosophy, and the other in need of money. It was you again, I am well enough aware, who introduced him once again to Hippias of Elis, from whom he learnt his "art of memory"; since which time he has become a very ardent lover, from inability to forget each lovely thing he sets his eyes on. And quite lately, if I am not mistaken, it was you who sounded in my ears such praise of our visitor from Heraclea, that first you made me thirst for his society, and then united us. For which indeed I am your debtor, since I find him a fine handsome fellow and true gentleman. And did you not, moreover, sing the praises of Aeschylus of Phlius in my ears and mine in his?—in fact, affected us so much by what you said, we fell in love and took to coursing wildly in pursuit of one another like two dogs upon a trail.

With such examples of your wonder-working skill before my eyes, I must suppose you are a first-rate matchmaker. For consider, a man with insight to discern two natures made to be of service to each other, and with power to make these same two people mutually enamoured! That is the sort of man, I take it, who should weld together states in friendship; cement alliances with gain to the contracting parties; and, in general, be found an acquisition to those several states; to friends and intimates, and partisans in war, a treasure worth possessing. But you, my friend, you got quite angry. One would suppose I had given you an evil name in calling you a first-rate matchmaker.

Yes (he answered meekly), but now I am calm. It is clear enough, if I possess these powers I shall find myself surcharged with spiritual riches.

In this fashion the cycle of the speeches was completed.

Life of Diogenes

By

Diogenes Laërtius

I. DIOGENES was a native of Sinope, the son of Tresius, a money-changer. And Diocles says that he was forced to flee from his native city, as his father kept the public bank there, and had adulterated the coinage. But Eubulides, in his essay on Diogenes, says, that it was Diogenes himself who did this, and that he was banished with his father. And, indeed, he himself, in his *Perdalus*, says of himself that he had adulterated the public money. Others say that he was one of the curators, and was persuaded by the artisans employed, and that he went to Delphi, or else to the oracle at Delos, and there consulted Apollo as to whether he should do what people were trying to persuade him to do; and that, as the god gave him permission to do so, Diogenes, not comprehending that the God meant that he might change the political customs of his country if he could, adulterated the coinage; and being detected, was banished, as some people say, but as other accounts have it, took the alarm and fled away of his own accord. Some again, say that he adulterated the money which he had received from his father; and that his father was thrown into prison and died there; but that Diogenes escaped and went to Delphi, and asked, not whether he might tamper with the coinage, but what he could do to become very celebrated, and that in consequence he received the oracular answer which I have mentioned.

II. And when he came to Athens he attached himself to Antisthenes; but as he repelled him, because he admitted no one; he at last forced his way to him by his pertinacity. And once, when he raised his stick at him, he put his head under it, and said, "Strike, for you will not find any stick hard enough to drive me away as long as you continue to speak." And from this time forth he was one of his pupils; and being an exile, he naturally betook himself to a simple mode of life.

III. And when, as Theophrastus tells us, in his *Megaric Philosopher*, he saw a mouse running about and not seeking for a bed, nor taking care to keep in the dark, nor looking for any of those things which appear enjoyable to such an animal, he found a remedy for his own poverty. He was, according to the account of some people, the first person who doubled up his cloak out of necessity, and who slept in it; and who carried a wallet, in which he kept his food; and who used whatever place was near for all sorts of purposes, eating, and sleeping, and conversing in it. In reference to which habit he used to say, pointing to the Colonnade of Jupiter, and to the Public Magazine, "that the Athenians had built him places to live in." Being attacked with illness, he supported himself with a staff; and after that he carried it continually, not indeed in the city, but whenever he was walking in the roads, together with his wallet, as Olympiodorus, the chief man of the Athenians tells us; and Polymeter, the orator, and Lysanias, the son of Eschorion, tell the same story. When he had written to someone to look out and get ready a small house for him, as he delayed to do it, he took a cask which he found in the Temple of Cybele, for his house, as he himself tells us in his letters. And during the summer he used to roll himself in the warm sand, but in winter he would embrace statues all covered with snow, practising himself, on every occasion, to endure anything.

IV. He was very violent in expressing his haughty disdain of others. He said that the school of Euclides was worthless. And he used to call Plato's dialogues pretentious. It was also a saying of his that the Dionysian games were a great marvel to fools; and that the demagogues were the ministers of the multitude. He used likewise to say, "that when in the course of his life he beheld pilots, and physicians, and philosophers, he thought man the wisest of all animals; but when again he beheld interpreters of dreams, and soothsayers, and those who listened to them, and men puffed up with glory or riches then he thought that there was not a more foolish animal than man." Another of his sayings was, "that he thought a man ought oftener to provide himself with a reason than with a halter." On one occasion, when he noticed Plato at a very costly entertainment tasting some olives, he said, "O you wise man! why, after having sailed to Sicily for the sake of such a feast, do you not now enjoy what you have before you?" And Plato replied, "By the Gods, Diogenes, while I was there I ate olives and all such things a great deal." Diogenes rejoined, "What then did you want to sail to Syracuse for? Did not Attica at that time produce any olives?" But Phavorinus, in his *Universal History*, tells this story of Aristippus. At another time he was eating dried figs, when Plato met him, and he said to him, "You may have a share of these;" and as he took some and ate them, he said, "I said that you might have a share of them, not that you might eat them all." On one occasion Plato had invited some friends who had come to him from Dionysius to a banquet, and Diogenes trampled on his carpets, and said, "Thus I trample on the empty pride of Plato;" and Plato made him answer, "How much arrogance are you displaying, O Diogenes! when you think that you are not arrogant at all." But, as others tell the story, Diogenes said, "Thus I trample on the pride of Plato;" and that Plato rejoined, "With quite as much pride yourself, Diogenes."

Sotion too, in his fourth book, states, that the Cynic made the following speech to Plato: Diogenes once asked him for some wine, and then for some dried figs; so he sent him an entire jar full; and Diogenes said to him, "Will you, if you are asked how many two and two make, answer twenty? In this way, you neither give with any reference to what you are asked for, nor do you answer with reference to the question put to you." He used also to ridicule him as an interminable talker.

When he was asked where in Greece he saw virtuous men; "Men," said he, "nowhere; but I see good boys in Lacedaemon."

On one occasion, when no one came to listen to him while he was discoursing seriously, he began to whistle. And then when people flocked round him, he reproached them for corning with eagerness to folly, but being lazy and indifferent about good things. One of his frequent sayings was, "That men contended with one another in punching and kicking, but that no one showed any emulation in the pursuit of virtue." He used to express his astonishment at the grammarians for being desirous to learn everything about the misfortunes of Ulysses, and being ignorant of their own. He used also to say, "That the musicians fitted the strings to the lyre properly, but left all the habits of their soul ill-arranged." And, "That mathematicians kept their eyes fixed on the sun and moon, and overlooked what was under their feet." "That orators were anxious to speak justly, but not at all about acting so." Also, "That misers blamed money, but were preposterously fond of it." He often condemned those who praise the just for being superior to money, but who at the same time are eager themselves for great riches. He was also very indignant at seeing men sacrifice to the Gods to procure good health, and yet at the sacrifice eating in a manner injurious to health. He often expressed his surprise at slaves, who, seeing their masters eating in a gluttonous manner, still do not themselves lay hands on any of the eatables. He would frequently praise those who were about to marry, and yet did not marry; or who were about to take a voyage, and yet did not take a voyage; or who were about to engage in affairs of state, and did not do so; and those who were about to rear children, yet did not rear any; and those who were preparing to take up their abode with princes, and yet did not take it up. One of his sayings was, "That one ought to hold out one's hand to a friend without closing the fingers."

Hermippus, in his *Sale of Diogenes*, says that he was taken prisoner and put up to be sold, and asked what he could do; and he answered, "Govern men." And so he bade the crier "give notice that if anyone wants to purchase a master, there is one here for him." When he was ordered not to sit down; "It makes no difference," said he, "for fish are sold, be where they may."

He used to say, that he wondered at men always ringing a dish or jar before buying it, but being content to judge of a man by his look alone. When Xeniades bought him, he said to him that he ought to obey him even though he was his slave; for that a physician or a pilot would find men to obey them even though they might be slaves.

V. And Eubulus says, in his essay entitled, *The Sale of Diogenes*, that he taught the children of Xeniades, after their other lessons, to ride, and shoot, and sling, and dart. And then in the Gymnasium he did not permit the trainer to exercise them after the fashion of athletes, but exercised them himself to just the degree sufficient to give them a good colour and good health. And the boys retained in their memory many sentences of poets and prose writers, and of Diogenes himself; and he used to give them a concise statement of everything in order to strengthen their memory; and at home he used to teach them to wait upon themselves, contenting themselves with plain food, and drinking water. And he accustomed them to cut their hair close, and to eschew ornament, and to go without tunics or shoes, and to keep silent, look-ing at nothing except themselves as they walked along. He used, also to take them out hunting; and they paid the greatest attention and re-spect to Diogenes himself, and spoke well of him to their parents.

VI. And the same author affirms, that he grew old in the house-hold of Xeniades, and that when he died he was buried by his sons, And that while he was living with him, Xeniades once asked him how he should bury him; and he said, "On my face;" and when he was asked why, he said, "Because, in a little while, everything will be turned upside down." And he said this because the Macedonians were already attaining power, and becoming a mighty people from having been very inconsiderable. Once, when a man had conducted him into a magnificent house, and had told him that he must not spit, after hawking a little, he spit in his face, saying that he could not find a worse place. But some tell this story of Aristippus. Once, he called out, "Holloa, men." And when some people gathered round him in consequence, he drove them away with his stick, saying, "I called men, and not dregs." This anecdote I have derived from Hecaton, in the first book of his *Apophthegms*. They also relate that Alexander said that if he had not been Alexander, he should have liked to be Di-ogenes. He used to call cripples, not those who were dumb and blind, but those who had no wallet. On one occasion he went half-shaved into an entertainment of young men, as Metrocles tells us in his *Apo-phthegms*, and so was beaten by them. And afterwards he wrote the names of all those who had beaten him, on a white tablet, and went about with the tablet round his neck, so as to expose them to insult, as they were generally condemned and reproached for their conduct.

He used to say that he was the hound of those who were praised; but that none of those who praised them dared to go out hunting with him. A man once said to him, "I conquered men at the Pythian games:" on which he said, "I conquer men, but you only conquer slaves." When some people said to him, "You are an old man, and should rest for the remainder of your life;" "Why so?" replied he, "suppose I had run a long distance, ought I to stop when I was near the end, and not rather press on?" Once, when he was invited to a banquet, he said that he would not come: for that the day before no one had thanked him for coming. He used to go bare foot through the snow, and to do a number of other things which have been already mentioned.

Once he attempted to eat raw meat, but he could not digest it. On one occasion he found Demosthenes, the orator, dining in an inn; and as he was slipping away, he said to him, "You will now be ever so much more in an inn." Once, when some strangers wished to see Demosthenes, he stretched out his middle finger, and said, "This is the great demagogue of the Athenian people." When someone had dropped a loaf, and was ashamed to pick it up again, he, wishing to give him a lesson, tied a cord round the neck of a bottle and dragged it all through the Ceramicus. He used to say, that he imitated the teachers of choruses, for that they spoke too loud, in order that the rest might catch the proper tone. Another of his sayings, was that most men were within a finger's breadth of being mad. If, then, any one were to walk along, stretching out his middle finger, he will seem to be mad; but if he puts out his fore finger, he will not be thought so. Another of his sayings was, that things of great value were often sold for nothing, and vice versa. Accordingly, that a statue would fetch three thousand drachmas, and a bushel of meal only two obols; and when Xeniades had bought him, he said to him, "Come, do what you are ordered to."

And when he said "The streams of sacred rivers now run backwards to their source!"

"Suppose," rejoined Diogenes, "you had been sick, and had bought a physician, could you refuse to be guided by him, and tell him "The streams of sacred rivers now run backwards to their source?"

Once a man came to him, and wished to study philosophy as his pupil; and he gave him a saperda and made him follow him. And as he from shame threw it away and departed, he soon afterwards met him and, laughing, said to him, "A saperda has dissolved your friendship for me." But Diocles tells this story in the following manner; that when some one said to him, "Give me a commission, Diogenes," he carried him off, and gave him a halfpenny worth of cheese to carry. And as he refused to carry it, "See," said Diogenes, "a halfpenny worth of cheese has broken off our friendship." On one occasion he saw a child drinking out of its hands, and so he threw away the cup which belonged to his wallet, saying, "That child has beaten me in simplicity." He also threw away his spoon, after seeing a boy, when he had broken his vessel, take up his lentils with a crust of bread. And he used to argue thus, "Everything belongs to the gods; and wise men are the friends of the gods. All things are in common among friends; therefore everything belongs to wise men." Once he saw a woman falling down before the Gods in an unbecoming attitude; he, wishing to cure her of her superstition, as Zoilus of Perga tells us, came up to her, and said, "Are you not afraid, woman, to be in such an indecent attitude, when some God may be behind you, for every place is full of him?" He consecrated a man to Esculapius, who was to ran up and beat all these who prostrated themselves with their faces to the ground: and he was in the habit of saying that the tragic curse had come upon him, for that he was houseless and city-less, a piteous exile from his dear native land; a wandering beggar, scraping a pittance poor from day to day.

And another of his sayings was that he opposed confidence to fortune, nature to law, and reason to suffering. Once, while he was sitting in the sun in the Craneum, Alexander was standing by, and said to him, "Ask any favour you choose of me." And he replied, "Get out of my light!"

On one occasion a man was reading some long passages, and when he came to the end of the book and showed that there was nothing more written, "Be of good cheer, my friends," exclaimed Diogenes, "I see land."

A man once proved to him syllogistically that he had horns, so he put his hand to his forehead and said, "I do not see them." And in a similar manner he replied to one who had been asserting that there was no such thing as motion, by getting up and walking away. When a man was talking about the heavenly bodies and meteors, "Pray how many days," said he to him, "is it since you came down from heaven?"

A profligate eunuch had written on his house, "Let no evil thing enter in."

"Where," said Diogenes, "is the master of the house going?"

After having anointed his feet with perfume, he said that the ointment from his head mounted up to heaven, and that from his feet up to his nose. When the Athenians entreated him to be initiated in the Eleusinian mysteries, and said that in the shades below the initiated had the best seats; "It will," he replied, "be an absurd thing if Egesi-laus and Epaminondas are to live in the mud, and some miserable wretches, who have been initiated, are to be in the islands of the blest." Some mice crept up to his table, and he said, "See, even Diog-enes maintains his favourites."

Once, when he was leaving the bath, and a man asked him whether many men were bathing, he said, "No;" but when a number of people came out, he confessed that there were a great many. When Plato called him a dog, he said, "Undoubtedly, for I have come back to those who sold me." Plato had said, "Man is a two-footed, feather-less animal," and was much praised for the definition; so Diogenes plucked a cock and brought it into his school, and said, "This is Pla-to's man." On which account this addition was made to the definition, "With broad flat nails." A man once asked him what was the proper time for supper, and he made answer, "If you are a rich man, whenev-er you please; and if you are a poor man, whenever you can." When he was at Megara he saw some sheep carefully covered over with skins, and the children running about naked; and so he said, "It is bet-ter at Megara to be a man's ram, than his son."

A man once struck him with a beam, and then said, "Take care."

"What," said he, "are you going to strike me again?"

He used to say that the demagogues were the servants of the peo-ple; and garlands the blossoms of glory. Having lighted a candle in the day time, he said, "I am looking for a man." On one occasion he stood under a fountain, and as the bystanders were pitying him, Plato, who was present, said to them, "If you wish really to show your pity for him, come away;" intimating that he was only acting thus out of a desire for notoriety. Once, when a man had struck him with his fist, he said, "O Hercules, what a strange thing that I should be walking about with a helmet on without knowing it!"

When Midias struck him with his fist and said, "There are three thousand drachmas for you;" the next day Diogenes took the cestus of a boxer and beat him soundly, and said, "There are three thousand drachmas for you."

When Lysias, the drug-seller, asked him whether he thought that there were any Gods: "How," said he, "can I help thinking so, when I consider you to be hated by them?" but some attribute this reply to Theodorus. Once he saw a man purifying himself by washing, and said to him, "Oh, wretched man, do not you know that as you cannot wash away blunders in grammar by purification, so, too, you can no more efface the errors of a life in that same manner?"

He used to say that men were wrong for complaining of fortune; for that they ask of the Gods what appear to be good things, not what are really so. And to those who were alarmed at dreams he said, that they did not regard what they do while they are awake, but make a great fuss about what they fancy they see while they are asleep. Once, at the Olympic games, when the herald proclaimed, "Dioxippus is the conqueror of men;" he said, "He is the conqueror of slaves, I am the conqueror of men."

He was greatly beloved by the Athenians; accordingly, when a youth had broken his cask they beat him, and gave Diogenes another. And Dionysius, the Stoic, says that after the battle of Charonea he was taken prisoner and brought to Philip; and being asked who he was, replied, "A spy, to spy upon your insatiability." And Philip marveled at him and let him go. When Perdiccas threatened that he would put him to death if he did not come to him, he replied, "That is nothing strange, for a scorpion or a tarantula could do as much: you had better threaten me that, if I kept away, you should be very happy." He used constantly to repeat with emphasis that an easy life had been given to man by the Gods, but that it had been overlaid by their seeking for honey, cheese-cakes, and unguents, and things of that sort.

On which account he said to a man, who had his shoes put on by his servant, "You are not thoroughly happy, unless he also wipes your nose for you; and he will do this, if you are crippled in your hands." On one occasion, when he had seen the authorities escort off one of the stewards who had stolen a goblet, he said, "The great thieves are carrying off the little thief." At another time, seeing a young man throwing stones at a cross, he said, "Well done, you will be sure to reach the mark." Once, too, some boys got round him and said, "We are taking care that you do not bite us;" but he said, "Be of good cheer, my boys, a dog does not eat beef." He saw a man giving himself airs because he was clad in a lion's skin, and said to him, "Do not go on disgracing the garb of nature." When people were speaking of the happiness of Calisthenes, and saying what splendid treatment he received from Alexander, he replied, "The man then is wretched, for he is forced to breakfast and dine whenever Alexander chooses."

When he was in want of money, he said that he reclaimed it from his friends and did not beg for it. On one occasion he was working with his hands in the market-place, and said, "I wish I could rub my stomach in the same way, and so avoid hunger." When he saw a young man going with some satraps to supper, he dragged him away and led him off to his relations, and bade them take care of him. He was once addressed by a youth beautifully adorned, who asked him some question; and he refused to give him any answer, till he satisfied him whether he was a man or a woman. And on one occasion, when a youth was playing the coitabus in the bath, he said to him, "The better you do it, the worse you do it." Once at a banquet, some of the guests threw him bones, as if he had been a dog; so he, as he went away, put up his leg against them as if he had been a dog in reality. He said that a rich but ignorant man was like a sheep with a golden fleece. When he saw a notice on the house of a profligate man, "To be sold." "I knew," said he, "that you who are so incessantly drunk, would soon vomit up your owner." To a young man, who was complaining of the number of people who sought his acquaintance, he said, "Do not make such a parade of your vanity." Having been in a very dirty bath, he said, "I wonder where the people, who bathe here, clean themselves." When all the company was blaming an indifferent harp-player, he alone praised him, and being asked why he did so, he said, "Because, though he is such as he is, he plays the harp and does not steal." He saluted a harp player who was always left alone by his hearers, with, "Good morning, cock;" and when the man asked him, "Why so?" he said, "Because you, when you sing, make everyone get up." When a young man was one day making a display of himself, he, having filled the bosom of his robe with lupins, began to eat them; and when the multitude looked at him, he said, "that he marveled at their leaving the young man to look at him." And when a man, who was very superstitious, said to him, "With one blow I will break your head;" "And I," he replied, "with one sneeze will make you tremble." When Hegesias entreated him to lend him one of his books, he said, "You are a silly fellow, Hegesias, for you will not take painted figs, but real ones; and yet you overlook the genuine practice of virtue, and seek for what is merely written." A man once reproached him with his banishment, and his answer was, "You wretched man, that is what made me a philosopher." And when, on another occasion, some one said to him, "The people of Sinope condemned you to banishment," he replied, "And I condemned them to remain where they were." Once he saw a man who had been victor at the Olympic games, feeding sheep, and he said to him, "You have soon come across my friend from the Olympic games, to the Nemean."

When he was asked why athletes are insensible to pain, he said, "Because they are built up of pork and beef." He once asked for a statue; and being questioned as to his reason for doing so, he said, "I am practising disappointment." Once he was begging of some one (for he did this at first out of actual want), he said, "If you have given to anyone else, give also to me; and if you have never given to any one, then begin with me." On one occasion, he was asked by the tyrant, "What sort of brass was the best for a statue?" and he replied, "That of which the statues of Harmodius and Aristogiton are made." When he was asked how Dionysius treats his friends, he said, "Like bags; those which are full he hangs up, and those which are empty he throws away." A man who was lately married put an inscription on his house, "Hercules Callinicus, the son of Jupiter, lives here; let no evil enter." And so Diogenes wrote in addition, "An alliance is made after the war is over." He used to say that covetousness was the metropolis of all evils. Seeing on one occasion a profligate man in an inn eating olives, he said, "If you had dined thus, you would not have supped thus." One of his apothegms was, that good men were the images of the Gods; another, that love was the business of those who had nothing to do. When he was asked what was miserable in life, he answered, "An indigent old man." And when the question was put to him, what beast inflicts the worst bite, he said, "Of wild beasts the sycophant, and of tame animals the flatterer."

On one occasion he saw two Centaurs very badly painted; he said, "Which of the two is the worst?" He used to say that a speech, the object of which was solely to please, was a honeyed halter. He called the belly, the Charybdis of life. Having heard once that Didymon the adulterer, had been caught in the fact, he said, "He deserves to be hung by his name." When the question was put to him, why gold is of a pale colour, he said, "Because it has so many people plotting."

When he saw a woman in a litter, he said, "The cage is not suited to the animal." And seeing a runaway slave sitting on a well, he said, "My boy, take care you do not fall in." Another time, he saw a little boy who was a stealer of clothes from the baths, and said, " Are you going for unguents, or for other garments. Seeing some women hanging on olive trees, he said, "I wish every tree bore similar fruit." At another time, he saw a clothes' stealer, and addressed him thus: "What moves thee, say, when sleep has clos'd the sight, To roam the silent fields in dead of night? Art thou some wretch by hopes of plunder led, Through heaps of carnage to despoil the dead?"

When he was asked whether he had any girl or boy to wait on him, he said, "No." And as his questioner asked further, "If then you die, who will bury you?" He replied, "Whoever wants my house." Seeing a handsome youth sleeping without any protection, he nudged him, and said, "Wake up: Mix'd with the vulgar shall thy fate be found, Pierc'd in the back, a vile dishonest wound. "

When Plato was discoursing about his "ideas," and using the nouns "tableness" and "cupness;" "I, Plato!" interrupted Diogenes, "see a table and a cup, but I see no table-ness or cupness." Plato made answer, "That is natural enough, for you have eyes, by which a cup and a table are contemplated; but you have not intellect, by which tableness and cupness are seen."

On one occasion, he was asked by a certain person, "What sort of a man, Diogenes, do you think Socrates?" and he said, "A madman." Another time, the question was put to him, when a man ought to marry, and his reply was, "Young men ought not to marry yet, and old men never ought to marry at all." When asked what he would take to let a man give him a blow on the head?" he replied, "A helmet." Seeing a youth smartening himself up very carefully, he said to him, "If you are doing that for men, you are miserable; and if for women, you are profligate." Once he saw a youth blushing, and addressed him, "Courage, my boy, that is the complexion of virtue." Having once listened to two lawyers, he condemned them both; saying, "That the one had stolen the thing in question, and that the other had not lost it." When asked what wine he liked to drink, he said, "That which belongs to another." A man said to him one day, "Many people laugh at you." "But I," he replied, "am not laughed down." When a man said to him, that it was a bad thing to live; "Not to live," said he, "but to live badly." When some people were advising him to make search for a slave who had run away, he said, "It would be a very absurd thing for

Manes to be able to live without Diogenes, but for Diogenes not to be able to live without Manes."

When he was asked what sort of a dog he was, he replied, "When hungry, I am a dog of Melita; when satisfied, a Molossian; a sort which most of those who praise, do not like to take out hunting with them, because of the labour of keeping up with them; and in like manner, you cannot associate with me, from fear of the pain I give you." The question was put to him, whether wise men ate cheese-cakes, and he replied, "They eat everything, just as the rest of man-kind." When asked why people give to beggars and not to philosophers, he said, "Because they think it possible that they them-selves may become lame and blind, but they do not expect ever to turn out philosophers." He once begged of a covetous man, and as he was slow to give, he said, "Man, I am asking you for something to maintain me and not to bury me." When someone reproached him for having tampered with the coinage, he said, "There was a time when I was such a person as you are now; but there never was when you were such as I am now, and never will be." And to another person who reproached him on the same grounds, he said, "There were times when I did what I did not wish to, but that is not the case now." When he went to Myndus, he saw some very large gates, but the city was a small one, and so he said, "Oh men of Myndus, shut your gates, lest your city should steal out." On one occasion, he saw a man who had been detected stealing purple, and so he said:

A purple death, and mighty fate o'ertook him.

When Craterus entreated him to come and visit him, he said, "I would rather lick up salt at Athens, than enjoy a luxurious table with Craterus." On one occasion, he met Anaxirnenes, the orator, who was a fat man, and thus accosted him; "Pray give us, who are poor, some of your belly; for by so doing you will be relieved yourself, and you will assist us." And once, when he was discussing some point, Dioge-nes held up a piece of salt fish, and drew off the attention of his hearers; and as Anaximenes was indignant at this, he said, "See, one pennyworth of salt fish has put an end to the lecture of Anaximenes." Being once reproached for eating in the market-place, he made an-swer, "I did, for it was in the market-place that I was hungry." Some authors also attribute the following repartee to him. Plato saw him washing vegetables, and so, coming up to him, he quietly accosted him thus, "If you had paid court to Dionysius, you would not have been washing vegetables."

"And," he replied, with equal quietness, "if you had washed vegetables, you would never have paid court to Dionysius." When a man said to him once, "Most people laugh at you;" "And very likely," he replied, "the asses laugh at them; but they do not regard the asses, neither do I regard them." Once he saw a youth studying philosophy, and said to him, "Well done; inasmuch as you are leading those who admire your person to contemplate the beauty of your mind." A certain person was admiring the offerings in the temple at Samothrace, and he said to him, "They would have been much more numerous, if those who were lost had offered them instead of those who were saved; "but some attribute this speech to Diagoras the Thelian. Once he saw a handsome youth going to a banquet, and said to him, "You will come back worse;" and when he the next day after the banquet said to him, "I have left the banquet, and was no worse for it;" he replied, "You were not Chiron, but Eurytion."

He was begging once of a very ill-tempered man, and as he said to him, "If you can persuade me, I will give you something;" he replied, "If I could persuade you, I would beg you to hang yourself."

He was on one occasion returning from Lacedaemon to Athens; and when someone asked him, "Whither are you going, and whence do you come?" he said, "I am going from the men's apartments to the women's."

Another time he was returning from the Olympic games, and when someone asked him whether there had been a great multitude there, he said, "A great multitude, but very few men." He used to say that debauched men resembled figs growing on a precipice; the fruit of which is not tasted by men, but devoured by crows and vultures. When Phryne had dedicated a golden statue of Venus at Delphi, he wrote upon it, "From the profligacy of the Greeks."

Once Alexander the Great came and stood by him, and said, "I am Alexander, the great king." "And I," said he, "am Diogenes the dog." And when he was asked to what actions of his it was owing that he was called a dog, he said, "Because I fawn upon those who give me anything, and bark at those who give me nothing, and bite the rogues." On one occasion he was gathering some of the fruit of a fig-tree, and when the man who was guarding it told him a man hung himself on this tree the other day, "I, then," said he, "will now purify it." Once he saw a man who had been a conqueror at the Olympic games looking very often at a courtesan; "Look," said he, "at that war-like ram, who is taken prisoner by the first girl he meets." One of his sayings was, that good-looking courtesans were like poisoned mead.

On one occasion he was eating his dinner in the market place, and the bystanders kept constantly calling out "Dog;" but he said, "It is you who are the dogs, who stand around me while I am at dinner." When two effeminate fellows were getting out of his way, he said, "Do not be afraid, a dog does not eat beetroot." Seeing an unskilful wrestler professing to heal a man he said, "What are you about, are you in hopes now to overthrow those who formerly conquered you?" On one occasion he saw the son of a courtesan throwing a stone at a crowd, and said to him, "Take care, lest you hit your father." When a boy showed him a sword that he had received from one to whom he had done some discreditable service, he told him, "The sword is a good sword, but the handle is infamous." And when some people were praising a man who had given him something, he said to them, "And do not you praise me who was worthy to receive it?" He was asked by someone to give him back his cloak; but he replied, "If you gave it me, it is mine; and if you only lent it me, I am using it." A supposititious son of somebody once said to him, that he had gold in his cloak; "No doubt," said he, "that is the very reason why I sleep with it under my head." When he was asked what advantage he had derived from philosophy, he replied, "If no other, at least this, that I am prepared for every kind of fortune." The question was put to him what countryman he was, and he replied, "A Citizen of the world."

Some men were sacrificing to the Gods to prevail on them to send them sons, and he said, "And do you not sacrifice to procure sons of a particular character?" Once he was asking the president of a society for a contribution, and said to him: "Spoil all the rest, but keep your hands from Hector." He used to say that courtesans were the queens of kings; for that they asked them for whatever they chose. When the Athenians had voted that Alexander was Bacchus, he said to them, "Vote, too, that I am Serapis." When a man reproached him forgoing into unclean places, he said, "The sun too penetrates into privies, but is not polluted by them." When supping in a temple, as some dirty loaves were set before him, he took them up and threw them away, saying that nothing dirty ought to come into a temple; and when someone said to him, "You philosophize without being possessed of any knowledge," he said, "If I only pretend to wisdom, that is philosophizing." A man once brought him a boy, and said that he was a very clever child, and one of an admirable disposition." "What, then," said Diogenes, "does he want of me?" He used to say, that those who utter virtuous sentiments but do not do them, are no better than harps, for that a harp has no hearing or feeling. Once he was going into a theatre while everyone else was coming out of it; and when asked why he did so, "It is," said he, "what I have been doing all my life." Once when he saw a young man putting on effeminate airs, he said to him, "Are you not ashamed to have worse plans for yourself than nature had for you? for she has made you a man, but you are trying to force yourself to be a woman." When he saw an ignorant man tuning a psaltery, he said to him, "Are you not ashamed to be arranging proper sounds on a wooden instrument, and not arranging your soul to a proper life?" When a man said to him, "I am not calculated for philosophy," he said, "Why then do you live, if you have no desire to live properly?"

To a man who treated his father with contempt, he said, "Are you not ashamed to despise him to whom you owe it that you have it in your power to give yourself airs at all?" Seeing a handsome young man chattering in an unseemly manner, he said, "Are you not ashamed to draw a sword cut of lead out of a scabbard of ivory?" Being once reproached for drinking in a vintner's shop, he said, "I have my hair cut, too, in a barber's." At another time, he was attacked for having accepted a cloak from Antipater, but he replied: "Refuse not thou to heed the gifts which from the mighty Gods proceed."

A man once struck him with a broom, and said, "Take care;" so he struck him in return with his staff, and said, "Take care." He once said to a man who was addressing anxious entreaties to a courtesan, "What can you wish to obtain, you wretched man, that you had not better be disappointed in?" Seeing a man reeking all over with unguents, he said to him, "Have a care, lest the fragrance of your head give a bad odour to your life." He once asked a profligate fellow for a mina; and when he put the question to him, why he asked others for an obol, and him for a mina, he said, "Because I hope to get something from the others another time, but the Gods alone know whether I shall ever extract anything from you again." Once he was reproached for asking favours, while Plato never asked for any; and he said; "He asks as well as I do, but he does it bending his head, that no one else may hear."

One day he saw an unskilful archer shooting; so he went and sat down by the target, saying, "Now I shall be out of harm's way."

He used to say, that those who were in love were disappointed in regard of the pleasure they expected. When he was asked whether death was an evil, he replied, "How can that be an evil which we do not feel when it is present?" When Alexander was once standing by him, and saying, "Do not you fear me?" He replied, "No; for what are you, a good or an evil?" And as he said that he was good, "Who, then," said Diogenes, "fears the good?" He used to say, that education was, for the young sobriety, for the old comfort, for the poor riches, and for the rich an ornament."

When Didymus the adulterer was once trying to cure the eye of a young girl, he said, "Take care, lest when you are curing the eye of the maiden, you do not hurt the pupil." A man once said to him, that his friends laid plots against him; "What then," said he, "are you to do, if you must look upon both your friends and enemies in the same light?" On one occasion he was asked, what was the most excellent thing among men; and he said, "Freedom of speech." He went once into a school, and saw many statues of the Muses, but very few pupils, and said, "Gods, and all my good schoolmasters, you have plenty of pupils." He was in the habit of doing everything in public, whether in respect of Venus or Ceres; and he used to put his conclusions in this way to people: "If there is nothing absurd in dining, then it is not absurd to dine in the market-place. But it is not absurd to dine, therefore it is riot absurd to dine in the market-place." And as he was continually doing manual work in public, he said one day, "Would that by rubbing my belly I could get rid of hunger." Other sayings also are attributed to him, which it would take a long time to enumerate, there is such a multiplicity of them.

He used to say, that there were two kinds of exercise: that, namely, of the mind and that of the body; and that the latter of these created in the mind such quick and agile phantasies at the time of its performance, as very much facilitated the practice of virtue; but that one was imperfect without the other, since the health and vigour necessary for the practice of what is good, depend equally on both mind and body. And he used to allege as proofs of this, and of the ease which practice imparts to acts of virtue, that people could see that in the case of mere common working trades, and other employments of that kind, the artisans arrived at no inconsiderable accuracy by constant practice; and that any one may see how much one flute player, or one wrestler, is superior to another, by his own continued practice. And that if these men transferred the same training to their minds they would not labour in a profitless or imperfect manner. He used to say also, that there was nothing whatever in life which could be brought to perfection without practice, and that that alone was able to overcome every obstacle; that, therefore, as we ought to repudiate all useless toils, and to apply ourselves to useful labours, and to live happily, we are only unhappy in consequence of most exceeding folly. For the very contempt of pleasure, if we only inure ourselves to it, is very pleasant; and just as they who are accustomed to live luxuriously, are brought very unwillingly to adopt the contrary system; so they who have been originally inured to that opposite system, feel a sort of pleasure in the contempt of pleasure.

This used to be the language which he held, and he used to show in practice, really altering men's habits, arid deferring in all things rather to the principles of nature than to those of law; saying that he was adopting the same fashion of life as Hercules had, preferring nothing in the world to liberty; and saying that everything belonged to the wise, and advancing arguments such as I mentioned just above. For instance: everything belongs to the Gods; and the Gods are friends to the wise; and all the property of friends is held in common; therefore everything belong to the wise. He also argued about the law, that without it there is no possibility of a constitution being maintained; for without a city there can be nothing orderly, but a city is an orderly thing; and without a city there can be no law; therefore law is order. And he played in the same manner with the topics of noble birth, and reputation, and all things of that kind, saying that they were all veils, as it were, for wickedness; and that that was the only proper constitution which consisted, in order. Another of his doctrines was that all women ought to be possessed in common; and he said that marriage was a nullity, and that the proper way would be for every man to live with her whom he could persuade to agree with him. And on the same principle he said, that all people's sons ought to belong to everyone in common; and there was nothing intolerable in the idea of taking anything out of a temple, or eating any animal whatever, and that there was no impiety in tasting even human flesh; as is plain from the habits of foreign nations; and he said that this principle might be correctly extended to every case and every people. For lie said that in reality everything was a combination of all things. For that in bread there was meat, and in vegetables there was bread, and so there were some particles of all other bodies in everything, communicating by invisible passages and evaporating.

VII. And he explains this theory of his clearly in the Thyestes, if indeed the tragedies attributed to him are really his composition, and not rather the work of Philistus, his intimate friend, or of Pasiphon, the son of Lucian, who is stated by Phavorinus, in his Universal History, to have written them after Diogenes' death.

VIII. Music and geometry, and astronomy, and all things of that kind, he neglected, as useless and unnecessary. But he was a man very happy in meeting arguments, as is plain from what we have already said.

IX. And he bore being sold with a most magnanimous spirit. For as he was sailing and was taken prisoner by some pirates, under the command of Scirpalus, he was carried off to Crete and sold; and when the Circe asked him what art he understood, he said, "That of governing men." And presently pointing out a Corinthian, very carefully dressed, (the same Xeniades whom we have mentioned before), he said, "Sell me to that man; for he wants a master." Accordingly Xeniades bought him and carried him away to Corinth; and then he made him tutor of his sons, and committed to him the entire management of his house. And he behaved himself in every affair in such a manner, that Xeniades, when looking over his property, said, "A good genius has come into my house." And Cleomenes, in his book which is called *The Schoolmaster*, says, that he wished to ransom all his relations, but that Diogenes told him that they were all fools; for that lions did not become the slaves of those who kept them, but, on the contrary, those who maintained lions were their slaves. For that it was the part of a slave to fear, but that wild beasts were formidable to men.

X. And the man had the gift of persuasion in a wonderful degree; so that he could easily overcome any one by his arguments. Accordingly, it is said that a man of the name Onesicritus, having two sons, sent to Athens one of them, whose name was Androsthenes, and that he, after having heard Diogenes lecture, remained there; and that after that, he sent the elder, Philiscus, who has been already mentioned, and that Philiscus was charmed in the same manner. And last of all, he came himself, and then he too remained, no less than his son, studying philosophy at the feet of Diogenes. So great a charm was there in the discourses of Diogenes. Another pupil of his was Phocion, who was surnamed the Good; and Stilpon, the Megarian, and a great many other men of eminence as statesmen.

XI. He is said to have died when he was nearly ninety years of age, hut there are different accounts given of his death. For some say that he ate an ox's foot raw, and was in consequence seized with a bilious attack, of which he died; others, of whom Cercidas, a Megalopolitan or Cretan, is one, say that he died of holding his breath for several days; and Cercidas speaks thus of him in his *Meliambics*:

> *He, that Sinopian who bore the stick,*
> *Wore his cloak doubled, and in th' open air*
> *Dined without washing, would not bear with life*
> *A moment longer: but he shut his teeth,*
> *And held his breath. He truly was the son*
> *Of Jove, and a most heavenly-minded dog,*
> *The wise Diogenes.*

Others say that he, while intending to distribute a polypus to his dogs, was bitten by them through the tendon of his foot, and so died. But his own greatest friends, as Antisthenes tells us in his Successions, rather sanction the story of his having died from holding his breath. For he used to live in the Craneum, which was a Gymnasium at the gates of Corinth. And his friends came according to their custom, and found him with his head covered; and as they did not suppose that he was asleep, for he was not a man much subject to the influence of night or sleep, they drew away his cloak from his face, and found him no longer breathing; and they thought that he had done this on purpose, wishing to escape the remaining portion of his life.

On this there was a quarrel, as they say, between his friends, as to who should bury him, and they even came to blows; but when the elders and chief men of the city came there, they say that he was buried by them at the gate which leads to the Isthmus, And they placed over him a pillar, and on that a dog in Parian marble. And at a later period his fellow citizens honoured him with brazen statues, and put this inscription on them:

E'en brass by lapse of time doth old become,
But there is no such time as shall efface,
Your lasting glory, wise -- ,
Since you alone did teach to men the art
Of a contented life: the surest path
To glory and a lasting happiness.

We ourselves have also written an epigram on him in the proceleusmatic metre.

Tell me, Diogenes, tell me true, I pray,
How did you die; what fate to Pluto bore you?
The savage bite of an envious dog did kill me.

Some, however, say that when he was dying, he ordered his friends to throw his corpse away without burying it, so that every beast might tear it, or else to throw it into a ditch, and sprinkle a little dust over it. And others say that his injunctions were, that he should be thrown into the Ilissus; that so he might be useful to his brethren. But Demetrius, in his treatise *On Men of the Same Name*, says that Diogenes died in Corinth the same day that Alexander died in Babylon. And he was already an old man, as early as the hundred and thirteenth Olympiad.

XII. The following books are attributed to him. The dialogues entitled *The Cephalion*; *The Icthyas*; *The Jackdaw*; *The Leopard*; *The People of the Athenians*; *The Republic*; one called *Moral Art*; one on *Wealth*; one on *Love*; *The Theodorus*; *The Hypsias*; *The Aristarchus*; one on *Death*; a volume of *Letters*; seven *Tragedies*, *The Helen*, *The Thyestes*, *The Hercules*, *The Achilles*, *The Medea*, *The Chrysippus*, and *The Oedippus*. But Sosicrates, in the first book of his *Successions*, and Satyrus, in the fourth book of his *Lives*, both assert that none of all these are the genuine composition of Diogenes. And Satyrus affirms that the tragedies are the work of Philiscus, a friend of Dioge-Diogenes. But Sotion, in his seventh book, says that these are the only genuine works of Diogenes: a dialogue on *Virtue*; another on the *Good*; another on *Love*; *The Beggar; The Solmseus; The Leopard*; *The Cassander; The Cephalion*; and that *The Aristarchus, The Sisyphus, The Ganymede*, a volume of *Apophthegms*, and another of *Letters*, are all the work of Philiscus.

XIII. There were five persons of the name of Diogenes. The first a native of Apollonia, a natural philosopher; and the beginning of his treatise on *Natural Philosophy* is as follows: "It appears to me to be well for everyone who commences any kind of philosophical treatise, to lay down some undeniable principle to start with." The second was a Sicymian, who wrote an account of Peloponnesus. The third was the man of whom we have been speaking. The fourth was a Stoic, a native of Seleucia, but usually called a Baby-lonian, from the proximity of Seleucia to Babylon. The fifth was a native of Tarsus, who wrote on the subject of some questions concerning poetry which he endeavours to solve.

XIV. Athenodorus, in the eighth book of his *Conversations*, says, that the philosopher always had a shining appearance, from his habit of anointing himself.

Life of Crates

By

Diogenes Laërtius

I. CRATES was a Theban by birth, and the son of Ascondus. He also was one of the eminent disciples of the Cynic. But Hippobotus asserts that he was not a pupil of Diogenes, but of Bryson the Achaean.

II. There are the following sportive lines of his quoted:

The waves surround vain Peres' fruitful soil,
And fertile acres crown the sea-born isle;
Land which no parasite e'er dares invade,
Or lewd seducer of a hapless maid;
It bears figs, bread, thyme, garlic's savoury charms,
Gifts which ne'er tempt men to detested arms,
They 'd rather fight for gold than glory's dreams.

There is also an account-book of his much spoken of, which is drawn up in such terms as these:

Put down the cook for minas half a score,
Put down the doctor for a drachma more:
Five talents to the flatterer; some smoke
To the adviser, an obol and a cloak
For the philosopher; for the willing nymph,
A talent ....

He was also nicknamed Door-opener, because he used to enter every house and give the inmates advice. These lines, too, are his:

All this I learnt and pondered in my mind,
Drawing deep wisdom from the Muses kind,
But all the rest is vanity.

There is a line, too, which tells us that he gained from philosophy:

A peck of lupins, and to care for nobody.
This, too, is attributed to him:
Hunger checks love; and should it not, time does.
If both should fail you, then a halter choose.

III. He flourished about the hundred and thirteenth Olympiad.

IV. Antisthenes, in his *Successions*, says that he, having once, in a certain tragedy, seen Telephus holding a date basket, and in a miserable plight in other respects, betook himself to the Cynic philosophy; and having turned his patrimony into money (for he was of illustrious extraction), he collected three hundred talents by that means, and divided them among the citizens. And after that he devoted himself to philosophy with such eagerness, that even Philemon the comic poet mentions him. Accordingly he says:

And in the summer he'd a shaggy gown,
To inure himself to hardship: in the winter
He wore mere rags.

But Diocles says that it was Diogenes who persuaded him to discard all his estate and his flocks, and to throw his money into the sea; and he says further, that the house of Crates was destroyed by Alexander, and that of Hipparchia under Philip. And he would very frequently drive away with his staff those of his relations who came after him, and endeavoured to dissuade him from his design; and he remained immoveable.

V. Demetrius, the Magnesian, relates that he deposited his money with a banker, making an agreement with him, that if his sons turned out ordinary ignorant people, he was then to restore it to them; but if they became philosophers, then he was to divide it among the people, for that they, if they were philosophers, would have no need of anything. And Eratosthenes tells us that he had by Hipparchia, whom we shall mention hereafter, a son whose name was Pasicles, and that when he grew up, he took him to a brothel kept by a female slave, and told him that that was all the marriage that his father designed for him; but that marriages which resulted in adultery were themes for tragedians, and had exile and bloodshed for their prizes; and the marriages of those who lived with courtesans were subjects for the comic poets, and often produced madness as the result of debauchery and drunkenness.

VI. He had also a brother named Pasicles, a pupil of Euclides.

VII. Phavorinus, in the second book of his *Commentaries*, relates a witty saying of his; for he says, that once, when he was begging a favour of the master of a gymnasium, on the behalf of some acquaintance, he touched his thighs; and as he expressed his indignation at this, he said, "Why, do they not belong to you as well as your knees?" He used to say that it was impossible to find a man who had never done wrong, in the same way as there was always some worthless seed in a pomegranate. On one occasion he provoked Nicodromus, the harp-player, and received a black eye from him; so he put a plaster on his forehead and wrote upon it, "Nicodromus did this." He used to abuse prostitutes designedly, for the purpose of practising himself in enduring reproaches. When Demetrius Phalereus sent him some loaves and wine, he attacked him for his present, saying, "I wish that the fountains bore loaves;" and it is notorious that he was a water drinker.

He was once reproved by the sediles of the Athenians, for wearing fine linen, and so he replied, "I will show you Theophrastus also clad in fine linen." And as they did not believe him, he took them to a barber's shop, and showed him to them as he was being shaved. At Thebes he was once scourged by the master of the Gymnasium, (though some say it was by Euthycrates, at Corinth), and dragged out by the feet; but he did not care, and quoted the line: I feel, mighty chief, your matchless might, Dragged, foot first, downward from th' ethereal height. But Diocles says that it was by Menedemus, of Eretria, that he was dragged in this manner, for that as he was a handsome man, and supposed to be very obsequious to Asclepiades, the Phliasian, Crates touched his thighs and said, "Is Asclepiades within?" And Enedemus was very much offended, and dragged him out, as has been already said; and then Crates quoted the above-cited line.

VIII. Zeno, the Cittisean, in his *Apophthegms*, says, that he once sewed up a sheep's fleece in his cloak, without thinking of it; and he was a very ugly man, and one who excited laughter when he was taking exercise. And he used to say, when he put up his hands, "Courage, Crates, as far as your eyes and the rest of your body is concerned;

IX. "For you shall see those who now ridicule you, convulsed with disease, and envying your happiness, and accusing themselves of slothfulness." One of his sayings was, "That a man ought to study philosophy, up to the point of looking on generals and donkey-drivers in the same light." Another was, that those who live with flatterers, are as desolate as calves when in the company of wolves; for that neither the one nor the other are with those whom they ought to be, or their own kindred, but only with those who are plotting against them.

X. When he felt that he was dying, he made verses on himself, saying:

You're going, noble hunchback, you are going
To Pluto's realms, bent double by old age.

For he was humpbacked from age.

XI. When Alexander asked him whether he wished to see the restoration of his country, he said, "What would be the use of it? for perhaps some other Alexander would come at some future time and destroy it again. But poverty and dear obscurity, Are what a prudent man should think his country; For these e'en fortune can't deprive him of." He also said that he was:

A fellow countryman of wise Diogenes,
Whom even envy never had attacked.

Menander, in his *Twin-sister*, mentions him thus:

For you will walk with me wrapped in your cloak.

As his wife used to with the Cynic Crates.

XII. He gave his daughter to his pupils, as he himself used to say:

To have and keep on trial for a month.

Lightning Source UK Ltd.
Milton Keynes UK
UKHW020255100223
416720UK00002B/654